D1164799

An Introduction to Japanese Court Poetry

An Introduction
to Japanese Court Poetry

EARL MINER

With translations by the author and Robert H. Brower

Stanford University Press
Stanford, California
1968

Stanford University Press
Stanford, California
© 1968 by the Board of Trustees of the
Leland Stanford Junior University
Printed in the United States of America
L.C. 68-17138

For Geoff and Brian

Preface

A course of lectures at Oxford University in Hilary Term, 1967, was the immediate origin of this little book. But it had its earlier beginnings in the study of Japanese poetry, done with my friend Robert H. Brower, which led to *Japanese Court Poetry* (Stanford, 1961). Since the earlier book, I have reflected on the subject and have come to feel that literary preoccupations need to be tempered with attention to the fundamental human concerns of Japanese court poetry. It is these concerns that I have tried to emphasize here. In addition, I have sought to simplify and clarify much of what was presented in the earlier book by concentrating on the major poets and by treating their works, so far as possible, in a single discussion. This was relatively simple in the five chapters devoted to major poets, whose works require only a brief historical introduction to be appreciated. In the first two chapters and the last, however, the focus is more on trends and ideas than on individual writers.

Certain other emphases should be mentioned. Although "Japanese court poetry" means the serious poetry written in Japanese by members of the court or by others following their example, I have made no attempt at systematic discussion of the primitive songs surviving from preliterate to literate times. Because I believe them to be important more for historical reasons than for intrinsic human or literary interests, I have introduced them where their historical significance might illuminate the development of court poetry or the achievement of the major poets. Although such treatment of the primitive songs has curtailed my discussion of the earliest segment of court poetry, I have followed the example of modern Japanese scholars and pursued my subject to the beginning of the sixteenth century, bringing in a group of poets, mostly priests, who are at once successors to the court poets, court poets in their practice, and ancestors of the "feudal" poets of the succeeding era. The chronological range of this book is therefore from about A.D. 550 to 1500, with emphasis on the last eight centuries of that period.

My concern in this book is with poems, rather than social history, literary history, language, or biography. Of course, it has not been possible or desirable to ignore these subjects completely, but it is the poems that matter. The source of a given work is cited each time the work appears. At the risk of appearing pedantic in a book of this nature, I have decided to provide transliterations of the original Japanese for all the poems. I hope that this will give students with some Japanese a chance to approach the originals more nearly, and readers having more Japanese the opportunity to examine with care both the translations and my comments on the poems.

Nearly 160 poems or passages are included. The great majority are selected from *Japanese Court Poetry,* and about half of these have been revised. The revisions may amount to no more than the change of a single word or may involve a complete recasting. The purpose of the changes is to lessen the distance, in accuracy or effect, between the original and the English version. Thirteen poems are from a group of Japanese court poems translated by Professor Brower and myself and hitherto unpublished. Twenty-eight translations are my own. Since it would be altogether tedious to the reader to specify the provenance of each translation, I hope that this general statement will suffice and that any blemishes or inaccuracies will be attributed to me.

The appearance of better texts of the latter part of the *Man'yōshū* since our work for *Japanese Court Poetry* has enabled me to correct transliterations for a few poems.

I am very grateful to Professor Brower for our agreement that each may use or revise what both have done jointly. I also want to thank Professor Jin'ichi Konishi of Tokyo University of Education for his comments on some doubtful points. I am grateful to the curators and staff of the Oriental Institute of Oxford University for their courtesy and kindness, to the staff of the Institute library for valuable assistance, and to Professor David Hawkes, who allowed me the use of his office while he was away on sabbatical leave. I am grateful to the Committee on Research of the University of California, Los Angeles, for funds to prepare this book.

After writing the preceding paragraphs, I have had assistance in turning my manuscript into this book. I wish, therefore, to acknowledge with gratitude the aid of Miss Shoko Yoshimoto, who checked the texts and numbers of poems and the Finding List. Mr. John P. Loge, my research assistant, has once more proved his ability as a utility infielder in picking up, with his customary aplomb, the proofreading of a book on a subject out of his usual line. The value of such assistance is best known to me. But I think the reader will take the same pleasure in knowing, as I do in saying, that the book was designed by Mr. Richard Palmer, the art director of Stanford University Press.

The dedication bespeaks my gratitude and affection to two friends who helped make a year at Oxford especially gratifying to my family and to me.

E.M.

Los Angeles
April 1968

Contents

	Note on Abbreviations, Dates, and Pronunciation	xiii
ONE	Courtly and Human Values	1
TWO	Forms and Conventions	18
THREE	Hitomaro	36
FOUR	Major Poets from 686 to 784	55
FIVE	Major Poets from 784 to 1100	79
SIX	Major Poets from 1100 to 1241	101
SEVEN	Major Poets from 1241 to 1500	123
EIGHT	Major Themes	144
	Glossary	161
	Finding List for Poems	166
	Index	168

Note on Abbreviations, Dates, and Pronunciation

The following abbreviations or short citations are used throughout this book:

Azumaasobiuta "Songs for the Eastern Dances," numbered as in *Kodai Kayōshū*, ed. Y. Tsuchihashi and J. Konishi, Tokyo, 1957.

FGS *Fūgashū*, 17th imperial anthology, ca. 1345.

GSIS *Goshūishū*, 4th imperial anthology, 1086.

GSRJ *Gunsho Ruijū*, 30 vols., Tokyo, 1928–34.

GSS *Gosenshū*, 2nd imperial anthology, ca. 951.

GYS *Gyokuyōshū*, 14th imperial anthology, ca. 1313.

Kagura Shinto ceremonial songs, numbered as in Tsuchihashi and Konishi, *Kodai Kayōshū*.

KKS *Kokinshū*, 1st imperial anthology, ca. 905.

Kojiki An early chronicle (712) containing songs numbered as in Tsuchihashi and Konishi, *Kodai Kayōshū*.

K. Taikei *Kōchū Kokka Taikei*, 28 vols., Tokyo, 1927–31.

KYS *Kin'yōshū*, 5th imperial anthology, ca. 1127.

Monogatari Poems from tales, as numbered in the *Monogatari* section of *Kokka Taikan* (see paragraph immediately following).

MYS *Man'yōshū*, the great early collection of poetry, ca. 760.

Nihongi An early chronicle (720) containing songs numbered as in Tsuchihashi and Konishi, *Kodai Kayōshū*.

Nikki	Poems from diaries, as numbered in the *Nikki* section of *Kokka Taikan*.
NKGT	*Nihon Kagaku Taikei*, ed. N. Sasaki, 6 vols., Tokyo, 1935, and reprinted.
SCSS	*Shinchokusenshū*, 9th imperial anthology, ca. 1234.
SIS	*Shūishū*, 3rd imperial anthology, ?990–1005.
SKKS	*Shinkokinshū*, 8th imperial anthology, ca. 1206.
SZS	*Senzaishū*, 7th imperial anthology, ca. 1188.
ZGSRJ	*Zoku Gunsho Ruijū*, 71 vols., Tokyo, 1923–30.

The imperial anthologies, the *Man'yōshū*, and poems from the tales (*monogatari*) and diaries (*nikki*) will be found numbered in *Kokka Taikan*, ed. D. Matsushita and F. Watanabe, 2 vols., Tokyo, 1903, and often reprinted.

Citations of poems in the text refer to anthology or collection, to book or scroll number where appropriate, and to the number of the poem in the collection. "*MYS*, I: 1," therefore, refers to the first poem in the first book of the *Man'yōshū*. Citations of poems in *Gunsho Ruijū, Kōchū Kokka Taikei*, and *Zoku Gunsho Ruijū* refer to volume and page number (e.g., *K. Taikei*, XI, 98).

Even when not so indicated, dates are approximate. The dates of poets are given on first appearance and in the Index.

The poets are identified by their clan names and their given names or styles: e.g., Kakinomoto Hitomaro, Fujiwara Teika. They are later referred to by given names or styles: e.g., Hitomaro, Teika. Ranks and attributed appellations (i.e., acquired from a relative or from service) are given only for royalty, where other names are unknown, or where necessary to avoid confusion.

Transliterations of names or texts of poems have been normalized, where different, into modern equivalents.

Classical Japanese is constituted of lightly stressed syllables made up of a consonant and a vowel, a vowel, or *n*. Long vowels (e.g., ō) are counted as two syllables for prosodic purposes. The vowels are "pure" or "simple," as in Spanish or Italian. The consonants are pronounced very much as in English, except for *r*, which involves touching the forepart of the roof of the mouth lightly with the tongue to produce a sound combining some features of *l* and *d*. Pronouncing Japanese names or phrases with "pure" vowels, English consonants, and little stress will approximate the sound of the original.

For further discussion of these matters, and for a bibliography of Japanese sources and Western translations and criticism, see Robert H. Brower and Earl Miner, *Japanese Court Poetry* (Stanford, 1961), pp. xv, xvi, 489–502.

An Introduction to Japanese Court Poetry

CHAPTER ONE

Courtly and Human Values

What we designate Japanese court poetry is a historical segment (ca. 550–1500) of what Japanese themselves call *waka,* or Japanese poetry—serious verse written in their own language, as opposed to Chinese, from the earliest literate times. It was with the appearance of *waka* that the Japanese first became conscious that their poetry was a counterpart of Chinese or Korean, that it was their own possession, and that it was the product of their civilization. That consciousness or conviction serves as a useful point of departure in a discussion of court poetry, and no less because it is court poetry that defined the features of experience and expression that have dominated Japanese literature to modern times. The numerous changes in Japanese court poetry during the years 550–1500, which compare in length of time to the period from the Norman Conquest to the present, must be set aside for the moment. What we ought to discover, if possible, are the enduring characteristics of this lengthy tradition of Japanese poetry.

It would be foolish to presume that by reading the poetry alone we can infer the nature of the civilization that produced it. At a minimum, historical knowledge and tact are also required. Otherwise we may infer, as some educated Japanese have from our movies, that many Americans sleep with pistols under their pillows, or from Japanese films that most Japanese women are prostitutes. Reading Shakespeare's plays in such literal-minded innocence, we would be led to conclude that in his day Englishmen lived in enchanted forests, killed each other on little provocation, and spent their time making highly metaphorical speeches at court. It has been well said of the works of Emerson that they would give a visitor from another planet no conception that the human race comprised two sexes. We must be very careful to avoid too simple

I

inferences from Japanese court poetry, especially inferences founded upon acquaintance with too few poems.

It is also true that it is not possible simply to interpret the poetry out of the civilization that produced it. It is fallacious to assume that we need only feed into our imaginations or computers all the data about a civilization in order to show that its poetry must necessarily be thus-and-so. In the first place, we do not always have the data. For most of the court poetry period, we are ignorant of the domestic architecture of the nobility and of the lives of the poor. Even if we could recover enough information, our very scheme of computer programming would determine the results. And beyond that, the causes are so infinitely complex in their changing relations that the possible effects are infinite. To illustrate such difficulties, one may recall that during World War II someone in the Japanese government conceived the notion of having distinguished Japanese scholars prepare a "Patriotic Collection of Single Poems of a Hundred Poets" on the model of the very popular thirteenth-century anthology, *Hyakunin Isshu*, or *Single Poems of a Hundred Poets*. After painstaking effort the scholars reported back that they were extremely sorry, but from the thousands and thousands of extant poems they could not produce a hundred patriotic poems from classical poetry. Throughout recorded time Japanese have been patriotic and conscious of their national identity, but patriotism has not provided their poets with a literary option they cared to take up. Similarly, they have loved feminine beauty, and yet their love poetry does not describe, as Western poetry does, the features of the beloved. Izumi Shikibu does, it is true, speak of her dark hair (*kurogami*), but most of us might have guessed as much without her saying so. What we would not have imagined is the extent to which qualities of physical intimacy might be conveyed by an image like seaplants or diction like "the pillowing arm" (*tamakura*).

Still, a concern with the culture is useful in enabling us to approach, if but negatively at first, a major feature of Japanese court poetry: the fact that it reflects, in a special refraction, a *part* of its civilization. With some early exceptions, the poetry does not concern itself with the humdrum, the coarse, the economic, or the

2

sociological. Much that a courtier concerned himself with—abstinences, income, family power, political upheavals, intrigue, and so on—is treated, if at all, only obliquely in his poetry. As a person, he was deeply concerned about these matters, as we know from actual or fictional diaries and other sources. As a poet, he was deeply concerned with what he considered to be fit subjects for poetry. And what was fit? It is a perennial question in literature.

The model courtier in about A.D. 1000 was by education partly Shintoist, partly Buddhist, partly Taoist, and partly Confucian. When he, or she, essayed poetry, he ignored Confucianism and all that it implied about man's place in society and about abstract morality. He modified his already modified Taoism, usually by assimilating Taoist legends into a general classical fund. He wrote in a poetic diction (*utakotoba*) from which his Chinese loanwords had been refined away like dross. He became what was to him quintessentially poetic—and Japanese—putting aside the austere, businesslike Confucianism that in theory governed his society, and anything that seemed crass or coarse. Indeed he shed, with little apparent reluctance, abstract theory itself. He was interested in what he fancied was really poetry, not in what a Japanese once described as the crossword puzzles that make up English poetry. He turned his back on much that was important to him and sought what he believed to be higher ideals, what he would approvingly call courtly beauty (*miyabi*) or elegance (*fūryū*).

In other words, one of the most important characteristics of Japanese poetry to about 1500 is its courtly nature. The salient events in early Japanese history show how the court emerged. By the fourth century the country was sufficiently organized to mount raids, under the aegis of the throne, against the Korean states. Literacy was acquired by about 400, Buddhism by about 550, and constitutional precepts by about 600. Literacy and Buddhism enabled Japanese to view themselves in relation to other civilizations and their own past, as well as to acquire a proper metaphysics and complex moral philosophy. The constitutional precepts of Prince Shōtoku were a climax, a belated recognition that there was a working scheme of things centering on the throne. Each of these steps brought power and civilization into the hands of the group that could organize the state most effectively. But although the group in power changed repeatedly, it was always the sovereign who provided the charisma and validity of rule. What makes the period from about 550 to 1500 different from subsequent centuries is the fact that in it the court was a real political and social force. In the middle of the fourteenth century, Emperor Go-Daigo asserted imperial authority, not strongly enough to make the monarch a complete sovereign, which he had practically never been, but enough to show that power could rally about him. And Go-Daigo was even of doubtful legitimacy as a ruler. But beyond such dynastic power struggles there is for poetry the more significant fact that the civilization was defined in terms of its relation to the court and was the product of courtiers. In the last century or so of the period we are considering, there was a gradual shift in the identity of the effective artistic creators. But it may equally be said that to this day Japanese aesthetic perceptions and Japanese views on such matters as the true nature of love derive essentially from the court traditions of a thousand years ago.

In their own day courtiers thought that there were two significant ways of publishing poetry: the imperial anthologies (*chokusenshū*) and the poetry matches (*utaawase*) and sequences commissioned by the high nobility. Poetry also circulated in manuscript, and in everyday life there was an astonishing degree of poetic allusion and recitation, at least if we can trust the evidence of diaries and tales. But it was to the court itself that Japanese looked for immortality. Legends hold that men would risk their lives to win in poetry contests, or women their virtue to have a poem included in an imperial collection. Long before the court had reached the zenith of its political power, it was seen as the center of aesthetic possibility and authority. Long after the court had ceased to exercise effective political sway, its courtiers were envied, cajoled, and emulated for their priceless possession of the elements of civilization.

The dominant attitude toward court civilization in the great early collection, the *Man'yōshū,* appears to be that of an awed but happy wonder for what has somehow come into being and for what one has actually seen oneself. Yamabe Akahito (d. ?736) expresses the feeling clearly (*MYS,* VI: 1001).

4

Masurao wa	The noble warriors
Mikari ni tatashi	Set forth upon the royal hunt,
Otomera wa	While their ladies
Akamo susobiku	Trail their scarlet skirts
Kiyoki hamabi o.	Along the clean-swept beach.

Even personal poetry of the time is apt to reveal a consciousness of the court, as is shown by a passage from Ōtomo Yakamochi's (718–85) "Expressing My Own Thoughts" (*MYS*, XX: 4360).

Unabara mireba	When I look upon the great sea plain,
Shiranami no	Where the whitecaps
Yae oru ga ue ni	Splash about upon each other,
Ama obune	I see the fishing boats
Harara ni ukite	Bobbing here and there afar
Ōmike ni	As they gather in
Tsukaematsuru to	Food for the imperial table—
Ochikochi ni	Yes, widely scattered,
Izaritsurikeri.	The boats are fishing on the sea!

Perhaps the best evidence of all for the courtly consciousness of the poets included in the *Man'yōshū* is, however, the public poetry they wrote—on the deaths of princes, for example, or the discovery of gold. Kakinomoto Hitomaro (fl. ca. 680–700), the greatest poet of the age, popularized for longer poems a kind of poetic overture in which the nation's past and divinity were extolled. There are many poems in the *Man'yōshū* composed by provincials or by the humble; such variety is a happy feature of the collection. But the poetry of merit, the poetry that may be said like a wine to travel well, is the work of courtiers. In fact, civilization spread from the court to the provinces, and those who could not claim to be citizens of the capital imitated courtly attitudes as best they could.

The period from about 794, when the capital was established at Heian Kyō (Kyoto), to about 1156, when Taira Kiyomori became the first military figure to seize effective control of the court, may be taken as the characteristic period of the Japanese court. Its apogee of power was a shorter period, but one cannot fail to be struck by the fact that the court is, in the pages of the historians, as long in declining as, in the West, the middle classes are in rising. During the period of decline, the emperor continued to reign, the arts remained the same in basic assumption and form, and the courtiers continued to hold possession of the formal practice of rule and of poetry. How far the court was regarded as the center of civilization till 1500 can only be understood by the complete indifference to any alternative. In 905, the first of the imperial anthologies, the *Kokinshū,* included one book of travel poems. To the poets, travel (*tabi*) was by definition away from the capital and all it represented. The essential nature (*hon'i*) of the experience, therefore, came to be expressed poetically as a depression and misery commonly tinged with beauty. Of course, people journeyed back as well as away, but that was not *tabi*; that was "coming up" or "returning." The first work of Japanese fictional prose, *The Tosa Diary* (ca. 935) of Ki no Tsurayuki (868–945), treats the return to the capital of a provincial governor and his party (and therefore their journey is not called *tabi*). They cross the western border of the capital, the Katsura River, composing poems. For example (*Nikki,* no. 56):

Amagumo no	Katsura River,
Haruka naritsuru	All this time as distant to my mind
Katsuragawa	As high-floating clouds,
Sode o hidete mo	Though your waves have wet my sleeves,
Watarinuru kana.	Am I not crossed at last to home?

The woman imagined to be keeping the *Diary* comments, "Since it had become dark, we were unable to see the various places we had hoped to. Yet how good it is to be back in the capital!" In other words, they knew its value so well that they did not even have to see it.

Beginning about 1150 a new tone of loss comes into poetry, harmonizing with the nostalgia for the past that had emerged even in the *Man'yōshū* some four centuries earlier. Fujiwara Yoshitsune (1169–1206), who had the title of regent but not the power—the military had seized that—was in a good position to write about the nostalgia the court was feeling. His poem, "Mist at the Site of a Former Capital" (*K. Taikei,* XI, 98), illustrates the new attitude well.

6

Yamato ka mo	Once Yamato's glory,
Shikishima no miya	Our capital that stood at Shikishima
Shikishinobu	Wrings my yearning heart,
Mukashi o itodo	As with the grandeur of our past
Kiri ya hedaten.	It fades into the deepening mist of time.

Even poems in an auspicious or congratulatory vein may employ a lonely speaker reflecting on the past. Fujiwara Shunzei (1114–1204) furnishes an example in his poem to the god of the Hie Shrine (*SKKS*, I: 16).

Sazanami ya	Ceaseless its waves,
Shiga no hamamatsu	The beach of Shiga stands with pines
Furinikeri	Grown to glorious age—
Ta ga yo ni hikeru	How far past, the festivals of the New
Nenobi naru ran.	Year's planting
	When these trees were set as saplings for the god?

Another poem by Yoshitsune concerns autumn at the Fuwa Barrier, which was in ruins by his time, though its name means something like "The Indestructible" (*SKKS*, XVII: 1599).

Hito sumanu	The plank-roofed halls
Fuwa no sekiya no	Of the barrier fort of Fuwa "The En-
Itabisashi	during"
Arenishi nochi wa	Are emptied of their men,
Tada aki no kaze.	And in the ruin of all that was before,
	Only the rustle of the autumn wind.

Such early and later examples show that whereas attitudes toward the court undergo changes in the course of time, what does not change is the assumption of the courtliness of poetry, the belief that civilization resides with an emperor and his surrounding courtiers. The tendency can be seen even in the early historical records, the *Kojiki* (712) and the *Nihongi* (720), where old songs innocent of any dynastic intent whatsoever are interpreted as allegories of the divine origin of the state. Earlier neutral materials are made to serve the myth of divinity for an emergent court. And the same assumption of courtly hegemony in the arts can be exampled by the fact that in 1433 the shogun Ashikaga Yoshinori successfully requested Emperor Go-Hanazono (r. 1429–64) to commission the twenty-first—and, in the event, the last—of the imperial anthologies. Its title was to be *Shinshokukokinshū,* or *New Collection of Ancient and Modern Times Continued,* in conscious echo especially of the first of the "collections of twenty-one eras" (*nijūichidaishū*), the *Kokinshū,* or *Collection of Ancient and Modern Times,* completed more than five hundred years earlier. We shall subsequently have occasion to observe that the assumptions of the court poets were to have an effect long after new forms of government arose. This could only have been possible if the court had discovered certain essential truths about the civilization and had found ways of expressing these truths in literature. In addition to creating the greatest poetry and prose fiction the nation has yet known, the court established once and for all the sensibility that the Japanese themselves regard as particularly Japanese.

The influence of the court can be seen most readily in the imperial anthologies. The first major group of poems in each of them follows in broad outline both the sequence of the seasons and man's experience of nature as it was incorporated by court ceremony and liturgy into the Annual Ceremonial (*nenchūgyōji*). The other major group of poems concerns courtly love, with wooing in dim villas and alternations of poems between the aristocratic principals. The courtliness is revealed in such other sections as that of the travel poems already mentioned, that of the congratulatory poems addressed to the throne and the high nobility, and that of the poems of personal grievance (*jukkai*), usually expressing unhappiness at being passed over for promotion at court. Poems by humble frontier guards (often revised or ghostwritten by courtiers) appear in the *Man'yōshū.* Poems by such of the lowly as prostitutes or soldiers appear in later collections. But to write poetry meant to accept the subjects, language, treatment, assumptions, and canons of the court.

A court poetry is a poetry which is an accomplishment of courtiers, which takes its origin as a grace and social form in their lives. Classical Japanese poetry is not, however, merely courtly, and its

8

other characteristics require some discussion lest we assume merely that the poetry consisted of elegant little notes passed from Lord A to Lady B. Any gross contrast involves simplification, but it is broadly true that the faith which underlies Japanese poetry is different from that underlying Western literature. Their common elements aside, Western literature by comparison reveals a faith in action, in ideas, and in moral responsibility—these are what matter. Japanese literature emphasizes human feeling and reflection in participation with much that we think is opposed to man—especially nature and the divine. The contrast, if simplified more, is between Western faith in persuasive ideas and Japanese faith in cultivated feeling. To this extent, the characteristic figure of classical Western literature is the orator, and of Japanese the diarist. Quintilian's *Institutes* are as symbolic to the one as the calendar to the other; one literature seeks eloquence to comment on experience, and the other a scheme in which experience can make its own claims.

Faith in human feeling—belief in its integrity and truth—is probably the most consistent feature of Japanese literature from earliest to contemporary times. In the first Japanese critical document, the Preface to the *Kokinshū*, Ki no Tsurayuki expressed this conviction in his opening sentences, in which the central idea is that Japanese poetry "has its root in the human heart"; he reiterates the conception in his *Tosa Diary*, where the narrator says at one point, "Surely both in China and in Japan, art is what we create when we are unable to suppress our feelings." In a better-known passage of *The Tale of Genji* the same idea is expressed. As Arthur Waley translated it (Pt. III, ch. i), Prince Genji says in part that a person writes because his "own experience of men and things, whether for good or ill—not only what he has passed through himself, but even events which he has only witnessed or been told of—has moved him to an emotion so passionate that he can no longer keep it shut up in his heart." The doctrine resembles Wordsworth's conception of poetry as something resulting from the overflow of powerful feeling. But to Japanese, poetry is less the overspill of welling emotion than it is the constant current of feeling.

The respect accorded to correct or original ideas in the West has always been given in Japan to propriety or sincerity of feeling. And just as someone without an idea in his head is archetypally out of our civilization, so the person without a true feeling in his heart is archetypally out of the Japanese. In Japan, the person with most sensitive and best conducted feelings is considered superior to others. As Ki no Tomonori (fl. ca. 890) put it in a poem sent to someone with plum blossoms (*KKS*, I: 38):

Kimi narade	I am at a loss
Tare ni ka misen	To say to whom if not to you
Ume no hana	I might show these flowers;
Iro o mo ka o mo	For such beauty and such fragrance
Shiru hito zo shiru.	Only the best judge is a judge at all.

The knowledge or judgment possessed (*shiru hito zo shiru*), we may be sure, is a matter not of science but of sensibility. If such cultivated feeling is the best thing, then feeling itself is admirable. A very generous poem in *The Diary of Izumi Shikibu* (*Nikki*, no. 561) illustrates the belief that strong feelings, even those that are dubious by codes of official morality, do not incur the wrath of the gods. When her princely lover wrote protesting affection but failed to visit her, the Lady replied with a tinge of irritation, quoting very appositely a poem from *The Tales of Ise* (*Ise Monogatari*, 146; *Nikki*, no. 561).

Koishikuba	If I am so dear,
Kite mo miyo kashi	Why do you not come to see me?
Chihayaburu	Mighty they may be,
Kami no isamuru	The gods, but their injunctions
Michi naranaku ni.	Do not prohibit lovers' nights.

The faith in feeling was amply recognized by the writers and the critics. Diaries and tales repeatedly use the words *aware, okashi,* and *omoshiroshi*—all of them suggesting richness and intensity of feeling, whether in depth or novelty. (Of course, adjectives of feeling abound, often to the despair of the translator, puzzling over yet another word he may lamely render "sad.") Each of the terms has a long history of changing use, but during the period of the court the most important of the three, *aware*, describes feelings at once strong, irresistible to a person of cultivation, and natural to man. Usually *aware* has a strong hue of sadness, but sometimes it is used to indicate an intense experience of joy. Fujiwara Teika (1162–1241) advocated a poetic ideal he expressed in terms of "possessing heart" (*ushin, kokoro ari*); to him the essential condition of poetry was integrity of feeling, what he called "conviction of feeling." He went so far as to insist that, although there was one single style of "conviction of feeling" among the ten he named, the other nine styles he identified also required the same integrity of feeling. The courtly nature of poetry gave the poets the terms for their art. But the poets themselves believed that they would not have written—and no poet anywhere would have written—if they had not spontaneously, as well as by education, felt deeply and truly. Courtliness and feeling are therefore to some extent a polarity or a paradoxical set of values. One suggested what man acquired by civilized life, the other what was natural to him in being human. A similar and most creative tension in court poetry can be discovered by consideration of what were the motives of poetry. These were not the pleasure and profit of the Horatian ideal, but what may be called celebration and desolation. The faith in feeling not unnaturally led to a desire to celebrate those things that aroused feeling—perhaps seasonal beauties, perhaps travel, perhaps feminine attractions. The desire to celebrate the world one lives in is one of the oldest and most attractive features of Japanese civilization, and, although many elements would necessarily enter into a full account of the motive, no doubt the simplest way to account for this happiness and almost ritual praise of things is to point to Shinto, the way of *kami*, the indigenous spirits or gods. It will be recalled that these generous beings do not prohibit lovers' nights. In this they may have saved themselves from hypocrisy, because according to the chronicles they liked their pleasures, too. Perhaps it is peculiarly Japanese to believe that what is open to the gods is open to man. Indeed, it is notoriously difficult to draw the line between men and *kami*. The Shinto liturgy involved offerings of food and drink to put the *kami* in good humor. We can see this in the *kosaibari,* the oldest songs of the *kagura* ritual; these are amiable if not always clear in import (*Kagura,* no. 47).

Ame naru hibari	You skylark in the heavens,
Yoriko ya hibari	O skylark, fly down here;
Tomikusa	Rich grasses,
Tomikusa mochite.	Rich grasses bear to me.

It is not clear whether this was originally a children's song, whether it was some kind of allegory, or whether it began with some wholly different function; but unquestionably in the *kagura* it gives the air of friendly relations among birds and men and *kami*. Another example, a song of praise of the mash liquor imbibed by early Japanese, shows how free an expression the celebration of feeling allowed (*Kojiki,* no. 49).

Susukori ga	Susukori brewed
Kamishi miki ni	This august heavy liquor,
Ware einikeri	And oh, how drunk I am!
Kotonagushi	On the evil-chasing,
Egushi ni	Laugh-giving liquor—
Ware einikeri.	And oh, how drunk I am!

From the early, preliterate period there have also survived poems in praise of places, a motif that is particularly Japanese. Many an exiled Japanese has written poems in the vein of an anonymous early poet (*Kojiki,* no. 58; *Nihongi,* no. 54).

Tsuginefu ya	Going up
Yamashirogawa o	The river of Yamashiro
Miya nobori	Of the rolling hills,
Wa ga noboreba	As I go upstream to Miya,
Aoni yoshi	Passing Nara,
Nara o sugi	Rich in colored earth,
Odate	Passing Yamato,
Yamato o sugi	Where the mountains rise like shields—
Waga	Oh, the land,
Migahoshikuni wa	The country that I long to see again,
Kazuraki Takamiya	Takamiya in Kazuraki,
Wagie no atari.	The country of my home!

It is doubtful that one could find many square kilometers of Japanese soil uncelebrated by some poet or versifier. By the same token, the common reed, humble birds like snipe, singing frogs, the lovelorn stag—all are celebrated in poetry. There is a touching little early piece taking pride in the author's own rather nondescript homeland among the "Songs for the Eastern Dances" (*Azumaasobiuta*, no. 8).

Ōhire ya	O Great Hire
Ohire no yama wa	And Little Hire Mountain, too!
Ya	*Ya!*
Yorite koso	When you come close by,
Yorite koso	When you come close by,
Yama wa yora nare	How splendid are these mountains—
Ya	*Ya!*
Tōme wa aredo.	Though not much to look at from afar.

The delight lasts throughout the period of court poetry and beyond. A poet like Teika could find beauty in simplicity without needing to celebrate the great natural symbols of spring and autumn (*SKKS*, IV: 363).

Miwataseba	As I look about—
Hana mo momiji mo	What need is there for cherry flowers
Nakarikeri	Or crimson leaves?
Ura no tomaya no	The inlet with its grass-thatched huts
Aki no yūgure.	Clustered in the growing autumn dusk.

Even the briefest experience could arouse celebration in poetry, as a poem by Reizei Tamehide (d. 1372) shows very well (*FGS*, VI: 563).

Inazuma no	Even in the flashing
Shibashi mo tomenu	Of the lightning that does not linger
Hikari ni mo	Even for a moment,
Kusaba no tsuyu no	The very number of the drops of rain
Kazu wa miekeri.	Could be counted on the leaves of plants.

Shintoism had its share of ritual taboos and defilements; nevertheless, from it Japanese have derived a pleasure in their world, a sense of being really at home in it, that people of few other countries can know.

Along with the tendency to celebrate what is so wonderful in the world goes a contrary experience of desolation. The anonymous poet praising Takamiya is an exile from it. Teika's clustered huts fade into the dark and return to human misery. Tamehide's lightning has ended almost as soon as it has begun. The most beautiful things pass; what was taken for reality turns out to be illusion; lovers are untrue; hope withers; men's best efforts are in vain. Examples of such hollowness in human experience abound in the imperial collections. Ōshikōchi Mitsune (fl. ca. 900) expressed it this way (*KKS*, VI: 329).

Yuki furite	The snow falls on,
Hito mo kayowanu	Covering the road where not a person
Michi nare ya	Comes to visit me—
Atohaka mo naku	And will I melt in lonely grief,
Omoikiyu ran.	Leaving no trace of my transitory life?

In the original there is a play on words involving in part the phrase *haka mo naku*—"unstable," "transitory." It will be recognized at once that this is a Buddhist concept, and indeed, although Buddhism can be a religion of hope, in practice its coloring of court literature was dark. One reason for this was that in Japanese Buddhism any attachment to this world, even that of parents for their children, was a threat to salvation, was a "darkness of the heart" (*kokoro no yami*). There was the Law to think about, deterministic causation or karma (*sukuse*). At one major point in *The Diary of Izumi Shikibu*, the heroine recognizes that she can only give in to karma (*sukuse ni makasete*). Karma or the Law is similarly a source of dark coloring in *The Tale of Genji*.

Buddhism only lightly—though unmistakably—colors the first period of Japanese poetry after the advent of literacy. Though it later had such more optimistic versions as those of the Zen priests who influenced poets from the thirteenth century, there is no question that its general effect was to darken court poetry. The pessimists had only to point, as pessimists always do, to history: they were living in the Last Period of the Law (*Mappō*), in which salvation was probably impossible. But for most people, Buddhism was less such a historical curse than a directive force, taking one's attention away from this world and directing it to the others beyond. What was dear here was illusion there. Loving another person might not offend the Shinto gods, but it might endanger one's chances of being reborn on the lotus. As Ariwara Narihira (825-

80) put it, man simply did not know where he stood (*KKS*, XIII: 646).

Kakikurasu	Through the blackest shadow
Kokoro no yami ni	Of the darkness of the heart I wander
Madoiniki	In bewilderment—
Yume utsutsu to wa	You who know the world of love, decide:
Yohito sadame yo.	Is my love reality or dream?

Prince Genji amid his splendors confronts the same darkness and, on her trip back to the capital, the woman narrator of *The Tosa Diary* returns again and again to the sudden loss of her daughter (*Nikki*, no. 41).

Wasuregai	I shall not pick
Hiroi shi mo seji	Shells of forgetfulness from the shore,
Shiratama o	Since what I treasure
Kouru o dani mo	Will be the little keepsake pebbles
Katami to omowan.	Whose whiteness tells of her I love.

Buddhism did not cause the girl to die—that is not the point—but it produced in many men and women an annihilation of the heart. The devout Buddhist was caught between joy in the world and a sense that it was illusion, between love of children and a dogma holding such love inimical to spiritual well-being. Buddhism taught that choice was possible but protest useless. Man yielded to karma, the most beautiful flowers fell, and eternity cast very long shadows upon time. It makes little sense to bring our conceptions of such genres as comedy, epic, or tragedy to Japanese poetry—not because the Japanese are incapable of, say, epic values, but because with the Western associations of terms like "epic" in mind we are apt to imagine the wrong kinds of experience. Certainly, just as their poetry shows Japanese responding to the world with spontaneous joy as a place in which man is fully at home, so also it shows a sense of human deprivation so strong as to be desolating. As the joy flowed from the purest native springs, the sense of deprivation rested on the firmest of religious and philosophical foundations.

It may seem remarkable to us that the two responses exist together, not only as themes that may be reconciled but also as norms of human experience so fundamental that they require each other for full expression of man's awareness of himself. In long works one moves from mood to mood, responding to experience that may be quite contradictory according to Western notions of decorum. Anyone who has seen *kabuki* acted will recall such a succession of feeling, up and down and up, back and forth and back again. But there is yet a further step, in which the two responses are mingled, harmonized, and made into a third and particularly Japanese mingling of tones. That which is most beautiful tends to be the most ethereal, the most humble, or the saddest. Or to put it differently, what is celebrated may be the least real, the least attractive immediately, the least happy. The beauty of *aware*, which struck the heart with such force, like the depths of mystery called *yūgen*, was usually a reminder of mutability and was sometimes a shaft of death. Although the secret of the combination of celebration and deprivation may be peculiarly Japanese, it is not difficult for us to appreciate it. On the other hand, even Japanese themselves have had difficulty explaining how these complex harmonies come about. Kamo no Chōmei (d. 1216) tried to get at the problem in his *Mumyōshō*, and his attempts at definition are at least suggestive (*NKGT*, III, 312).

> On an autumn evening . . . there is no color in the sky nor any sound, yet although we cannot give any definite reason for it, we are somehow moved to tears. The average person lacking in sensibility—he admires only the cherry blossoms and the scarlet autumn leaves that he can see with his own eyes. Or again, it is like the situation of a beautiful woman who, although she has cause for resentment, does not give vent to her feelings in words, but is only faintly discerned—at night, perhaps—to be in a profoundly distressed condition. The effect of such a discovery is far more painful and pathetic than if she had exhausted her vocabulary with jealous accusations or made a point of wringing out her tear-drenched sleeves to one's face.

It is clearly easier to postulate such an ideal of sensibility as *aware* or to feel the mysterious pathos of *yūgen* than it is to define either one, just as we can less soon say what the beauty of a dying scene consists in than we can respond to the beauty itself. The Priest Jakuren (d. 1202) put the matter very well (*SKKS*, IV: 361).

Sabishisa wa	Loneliness—
Sono iro to shi mo	The essential color of a beauty
Nakarikeri	Not to be defined:
Maki tatsu yama no	Over the dark evergreens, the dusk
Aki no yūgure.	That gathers on far autumn hills.

Many elements enter into the civilization of Japanese court poetry. Something might be said of economics and politics, of the nature of the language and the example of China. The latter pair will enter the story subsequently; the former is too complex and indirect for discussion here. But we have the basis for an understanding, even in terms of politics and economics, if we recognize the significance for literature of the courtly nature of the society that created it, if we appreciate that society's faith in the truth of human feeling, and if we understand its conviction that the world in which man finds himself deserves celebration and yet that a desolation sweeps through man's heart. Such terms of reference reveal the extent to which court poets were different from us and to what like us. They were writers who may teach us how better to discriminate, improving our capacities by advancing them not only in degree but also in kind. As a line translated earlier from Tomonori put it, "Only the best judge is a judge at all." It is such judgment, such discrimination in human responses, that lies at the heart of the civilization of Japanese court poetry.

CHAPTER TWO

Forms and Conventions

As the creative elements of a civilization provide the soil from which poetry springs and grows, so the forms and conventions used by the poets affect the flowering of the poetry. In the narrower sense, forms and conventions involve such basic matters as prosody and techniques; in the wider sense, they concern the cast of poetic expression as well as the when, the to whom, and the how poems are written. Both the narrower and the wider senses are important, and both are suggested by the famous opening words of Tsurayuki's Preface to the *Kokinshū* (ca. 905).

> The poetry of Japan has its roots in the human heart and flourishes in the countless leaves of words. Because human beings possess interests of so many kinds, it is in poetry that they give expression to the meditations of their hearts in terms of the sights appearing before their eyes and the sounds coming to their ears. Hearing the warbler sing among the blossoms and the frog in his fresh waters—is there any living being not given to song? It is poetry which, without exertion, moves heaven and earth, stirs the feelings of gods and spirits invisible to the eye, softens the relations between men and women, calms the hearts of fierce warriors.

Tsurayuki beautifully expresses his faith in human feeling and his belief in the spontaneous naturalness of Japanese poetry. Also, however unobtrusively, he introduces into Japanese criticism its two basic terms: *kotoba* and *kokoro*. *Kotoba* means words, diction, or the materials of poetry—"the sights appearing before [men's] eyes and the sounds coming to their ears" as well as the tools of the language, imagery, and phrasing. *Kokoro* means heart, spirit, feeling, or conception; to apply Dylan Thomas to Tsurayuki's plant metaphor, it is the force that through the green fuse drives the flower. It is what gives the poem its predication, what gives life to the materials. *Kotoba* and *kokoro* are not adequately translated as "words" and "heart," but the English words may be taken as guides to the forms and conventions familiar to court poets.

Kotoba reminds us of the obvious but by no means simple fact that Japanese court poetry is written in Japanese. Of course, the language is a prime element of the civilization which created the poetry. But it belongs to the forms and conventions as well, because it is an art language as well as a natural language. As a natural language, it is explored in the seventh and eighth centuries, refined into an art language in the ninth and tenth, and maintained thereafter in remarkable purity as the proper language of poetry. If it is doubtful that anyone spoke the art language, it is certain that it was the only proper medium of poetry.

As a natural or art language it is very unlike English at any stage of development. It consists of four parts of speech—nouns, verbs, adjectives, and particles. It has a syntax generally fixed in word order within clauses and phrases but very free in larger syntactic combinations. Verbs are governed by topics as well as by subjects.* It differs from English, and for that matter even from modern Japanese, in its complex inflections of verbs and adjectives. Linguistic considerations are apt to seem remote from literary matters, but a little reflection will show that they are in fact crucial. The verbs of eighth-century Japanese, for example, have been convincingly analyzed by Dr. Masako Yokoyama,† who has shown that their inflections include premodal and modal forms. She shows that there are nine premodal morphemes and fourteen modal morphemes. The verb *momijitarikeri,* which might be rendered "has turned crimson," consists of a base followed by sounds conveying action, duration, perfection, duration again, and a final indicative mood. In *nakenaku,* a base adjective is inflected with a

---

* "Topics" implies an indirect, as "subjects" a direct, grammatical connection with the verb. Topics are usually less explicit than subjects; they suggest involvement, but not necessarily participation, in an action or state.

† "The Inflections of 8th-Century Japanese," Supplement to *Language,* XXVI, no. 3 (July–Sept. 1950).

negative and a nominal; Dr. Yokoyama says that it means "the fact being not that there is not," which, however precise, is not very useful to the translator. Whatever difficulties these highly inflected verbs and adjectives may cause the translator, however, to the earlier court poets, they were a major, and particularly Japanese, poetic resource. It is less cause for surprise that poets from early times to about the eleventh century exploited vigorously this aspect of their language, since it is so rich and so important to linguistic experience, than it is that poets thereafter paid more attention to other resources.

The other chief resource is inevitably nouns. Whereas the verb is so highly inflected, the form of the noun is constant, its functions being indicated as in modern Japanese by postpositive particles. A model simple sentence might run: noun plus *wa* for topic, noun plus *no* or *ga* for subject, noun plus *wo* for object, and our busily inflected verb. In poetic practice, however, all the particles and both the topic and the subject might be dropped. Such a procedure is roughly equivalent to removing from any given paragraph or passage of English verse every pronoun and every other subject and then casually shuffling the clauses. In Japanese prose the effect is often daunting, as anyone knows who has tried to parse *The Tale of Genji*. Such a relatively simple work as *The Diary of Izumi Shikibu* contains one sentence of fifty-seven clauses involving two sections of dialogue alternated with two of thought. One of each belongs to the prince and one of each to the lady, neither of whom is specified. The poetry is often easier to grasp, once one has learnt the linguistic, formal, and conventional elements, because although these complicate the verbal texture they also direct its meaning Poems consisting mostly of nouns are easier than those emphasizing verbs; concrete language, whether of nouns or verbs, is easier than general language. Poems employing complex verbs and adjectives are apt to be not only more general but also more subjective; those emphasizing nouns are usually more sensuous and descriptive.

In considering actual poetic uses of language, one cannot always sustain a distinction between natural and art language. Nonetheless, the very courtliness of court poetry implies the degree to which Tsurayuki's "words" were apt to be art words, however spontaneous his "spirit" or "heart" might be. The exclusion of Chinese loanwords, which gradually entered prose and presumably also conversation, is an obvious decision of art, affecting the poetry by narrowing its range of abstraction and increasing its purity, its sensuousness, its rhythm, and indeed its loveliness. This purely Japanese medium was then gradually further refined to become a poetic diction and an armory of imagery and implication. For example, by convention, *kaeru kari,* "returning geese," meant spring geese going north to what was imagined their proper home. *Yamahototogisu,* "wood-thrush of the hills," was by convention the bird early in its summer season of song, still mostly a bird of isolated areas and fresh in its voice. Later, when it had moved down toward the level or the coast, its song was thought less beautiful, and it was less fit for poetry. There is nothing unnatural in either phrase, but the setting of language with ever deepening traditions of what words imply gradually created the *utakotoba* or diction of poetry which came increasingly to be an art language. As the *kotoba* or words became weightier, the *kokoro* or heart needed to become stronger to sustain poetry, lest the creativity of tradition harden into mere convention.

The prosody and the forms of court poetry are related to the language in ways too subtle for explanation. It is clear enough that Greek poetry is based on quantity, English on stress, and Japanese on syllables. It is also evident that each prosodic system is natural to its language, but it is very unclear why. The Japanese definition of syllabic line lengths into alternating fives and sevens seems very natural once it grows out of the formlessness of primitive song. But the cause of what seems natural is obscure, like the reason for the alexandrine in French poetry or the decasyllabic line in English. Some scholars have theorized that the fives and sevens derive from a Chinese example. Another theory is that the line forms suited ancient patterns of singing or chanting. But no one knows. About all that is certain is that in primitive song the only fixed prosodic features were the integrity of the line and the sense of shorter and longer lines (see pp. 12–13 above). It seems almost certain that about the time of the advent of writing the fives and sevens developed out of the earlier shorts and longs. Without a proper prosody to define them, primitive songs had only the integrity of the line and a few set schemes to distinguish the songs from prose. As a result, they tended to employ schemes at once rigid and simple in order to give direction to what otherwise would be formless.

In much of the poetry of the *Man'yōshū* we find the opposite: a fixed system of prosody and a limited number of forms, but a greater range of conception. The basic form is the *tanka,* a five-line form consisting of 31 syllables arranged 5, 7, 5, 7, 7. The expanded form of the *tanka* is the *chōka,* consisting of a larger number of fives and sevens in alternation and concluding with the couplet of sevens. The longest *chōka* in the *Man'yōshū* consists of only 149 lines (see pp. 40–44, below). In addition to the *tanka,* which are also used as envoys to the *chōka,* and the *chōka,* there are two or three other forms, all brief and none of any great historical or intrinsic importance. Perhaps the *sedōka* may be mentioned, if only to show that it, too, is a variation of the *tanka,* consisting of two sets of the last three lines of the *tanka*: 5, 7, 7; 5, 7, 7. After the *Man'yōshū* even this not very remarkable degree of formal variety was lost, and the *tanka* became the only form practiced by poets until the linked forms of *renga* and *haikai* developed from *tanka* sequences. Both in classical times and in the present, Japanese poets have had difficulty in forging a prosody from a language so fluid that it would not take the shape of usual moulds of verse. Meter and rhyme, like quantity, are out of the question because of the nature of the sound and stress patterns of Japanese. Syllabic units alone could do the job; and in fact, so free did the language prove that for centuries only one form, the *tanka,* seemed able to contain it.

In a similarly restricted sense, the conventions of Japanese court poetry (as distinguished from the rhetorical resources of poets the world over) are as few as its forms. One of the earliest of these to appear is the pillow-word (*makurakotoba*), a conventional attribute or epithet usually occupying the whole of a short (five-syllable) line and modifying a word, normally the first, in the next line. Some pillow-words are so old that their meanings have been lost; others have been coined within the last century. Anyone familiar with the usual analysis of such poetic "formulas" in other poetic traditions must find it odd that a conventional attribute might be coined so many centuries after the advent of literacy; indeed, a novel conventional attribute seems a contradiction in terms. Yet somebody has to invent such formulas—one does not get them from the world soul or the folk soul. (It is thought, for example, that Hitomaro created about half of the pillow-words he used.) It is not always clear, therefore, whether a given expression is a pillow-word, an ordinary image, or a place name. An expression is a pillow-word if it sounds like a pillow-word to enough people, if it relates in an appropriate way to the word or words that it may modify. It must also give the effect of being grammatically, rhetorically, or semantically bound in the poetic context. For example, *shirotae no* means "of white hemp" (or perhaps paper mulberry) and conveys associations of whiteness, purity, and beauty when used as a pillow-word bound to words like robe (*koromo*) or sleeve (*sode*). Yet it could also be used literally when not bound—that is, when not a pillow-word. Japanese scholars have sometimes suggested that pillow-words have no meaning, but the evidence implies the opposite. For example, the most familiar of all pillow-words is *ashihiki no* for *yama* (hills, mountains). The original meaning of the phrase is uncertain, though it appears to have something to do with reeds—strange as that may seem, since Japanese like ourselves associate reeds with lowlands and bodies of water. By the time of the *Kokinshū*, poets had created a new meaning by false etymology, rendering the phrase as "dragging the legs," or "footsore," to suggest the effort of climbing a slope. They would not have done so if they did not presume the expression had meaning.

A second convention is the pivot-word (*kakekotoba*), which came into use as the pillow-word became less important. It is much clearer in its workings than the pillow-word, but harder to convey in English. At one point in *The Diary of Izumi Shikibu*, the heroine is so depressed that she writes her not too constant lover, saying that she is wearied with living (*Nikki*, no. 449).

Fureba yo no	Time and rain fall on,
Itodo usa nomi	And with them all I come to know
Shiraruru ni	Is increasing misery,
Kyō no nagame ni	Oh, that the long rain of my thought
Mizu masaranan.	Would raise the waters and swallow me.

There are two pivot-words: *fureba,* meaning both "as rain falls" and "as time passes"; and *nagame,* meaning both "long rain" and something like "a revery of gazing." A poem by Tsurayuki (*KKS,* I: 22) employs both a pillow-word and a pivot-word.

Kasugano no	Do those girls set out
Wakana tsumi ni ya	On some excursion for young shoots,
Shirotae no	As so deliberately
Sode furihaete	They wave their white linen sleeves
Hito no yuku ran.	Toward the ancient fields of Kasuga?

The phrase "so deliberately / They wave" renders the pivot-word *furihaete, furi-* alone meaning "waving," and the whole expression, "deliberately." The pillow-word is "white linen" for "sleeves" (*Shirotae no / Sode*). Actually, as we have seen, the original material was probably much more humble, either hemp or paper mulberry, but Tsurayuki has created a pastoral scene with his girls dressed in white on a spring outing in the fields of the ancient capital of Nara. The pillow-word therefore suggests a quality of the antique or pastoral, while the pivot-word suggests complete femininity, at least from the male viewpoint, because such attractive waving of the sleeves can only be deliberate. These techniques are not always used so meaningfully, but the continuing use of the pillow-word in adapted circumstances shows that once Japanese poets had invented a technique, they discarded it only with the utmost reluctance.

Later poets developed other conventions and, like Tsurayuki, used old ones in fresh ways. For twelfth- and thirteenth-century poets, the most meaningful technique was *honkadori,* allusive variation, which had been used earlier but which they made their own. This convention involved echoing and alluding to older poems or other parts of the shared cultural tradition in such a way that the older meaning is added to, or harmonized with, one's own surface meaning. In Episode CXXIII of *The Tales of Ise,* Narihira writes to a woman in the village of Fukakusa (which means "deep grass"), saying he must leave her and wondering whether she will remain faithful. She replies with a protest of her fidelity and a plea for his constancy which is so moving that he

resolves to stay (*Monogatari,* nos. 221–22; see also *KKS,* XVIII:
971–72). His poem runs:

Toshi o hete	When I have gone
Sumikoshi sato o	From this village of Fukakusa,
Idete inaba	After all these years,
Itodo Fukakusa	Will its deep grass grow ever taller
No to ya narinan.	And it become a tangled moor?

She replies:

No to naraba	Though it become a moor,
Uzura to nakite	Like the quails I will raise my plaintive
Toshi wa hen	cry
Kari ni dani ya wa	As the long years pass,
Kimi wa kozaran.	For can it be that you will not come back,
	If only briefly for the falconing?

That romantic exchange lies behind a poem (*SZS,* IV: 258)
by Fujiwara Shunzei.

Yū sareba	As evening falls,
Nobe no akikaze	From along the moors the autumn wind
Mi ni shimite	Blows chill into the heart,
Uzura naku nari	And the quails raise their plaintive cry
Fukakusa no sato.	In the deep grass of Fukakusa village.

Shunzei's is an autumn poem. It gains in resonance and significance by the romance implied in the allusion. The sense of beauty
and desolation in autumn is heightened by allusion to a love affair
between the dashing Narihira and a woman whose very name is
lost and by locating the scene in a village that no longer existed.
It had become a moor, after all, and the quails replace the lovers.
To Shunzei, Narihira was a great poet, a romantic lover, and a
symbol of the fading grandeur of the nobility. The heart-chilling
autumn wind symbolizes, therefore, the loss that has been suffered,
and yet the symbol rises wholly unobtrusively from the descriptive surface of the poem. It remains an autumn, but an autumn
invested with history, with symbols, and with human love.

To consider Shunzei's use of *honkadori* in such terms is undoubtedly to conceive of conventions in a wider sense involving the "heart" as well as the "words" of poetry. We must return for a moment to the more restricted sense. In the thirteenth and four-teenth centuries a form of yoking or zeugma became popular. It resembles the pivot-word, since it is used in two overlapping syntactic orders. But it differs in retaining the same meaning in both functions, as a poem (*GYS*, III: 419) by Kyōgoku Tamekane (1254–1332) shows.

Eda ni moru	In their rareness,
Asahi no kage no	The rays of the morning sun
Sukunasa ni	Filter brightly through
Suzushisa fukaki	The branches where the coolness
Take no oku kana.	Is deep within the bamboo grove.

As the translation is meant to suggest, "deep" (*fukaki*) modifies both the coolness and the grove. Still another technique used at the time was reversal or perturbation of language, a kind of cata-chresis employed in a love poem (*FGS*, XI: 1036) by Empress Eifuku (1271–1342).

Kurenikeri	It has grown dark.
Ama tobu kumo no	If only I might send the question,
Yukiki ni mo	"Won't you come tonight?"
Koyoi ika ni to	—Send it to you across the heavens
Tsutaeteshi ga na.	By the come and go of clouds.

In English we expect a phrase like "the clouds that come and go," not the reverse.*

Such conventions are those peculiar to court poetry. Much might be added about Japanese versions of such other conventions as allegory or personification, but the special character of conventions, in such a narrower sense, is clear enough. The larger conventions, those that admit rather more of the heart as well as the words of poetry, are, finally, more important. Without question the most important are those that correct the frequent impression

---

* Normal (and poetic) Japanese usage would be "the go-and-come of clouds," rather than "the clouds that come and go" of English. Another such "abuse" of language is "the wind falls" instead of "the wind blows." What is involved may vary from an odd phrase to syntactic aberration, from cata-chresis to metaphorical conceit.

of court poetry as a literature of precious little fragments. There is no need to make imaginary virtues out of faults, but neither is there cause to make faults of real virtues. It is historically true that Japanese poetry showed a slow but constant tendency to fragmentation, to development of shorter and shorter units, until after the Meiji Restoration the *haiku* emerged, discrete in its seventeen syllables. More than that, no *chōka* ("long poem") is as long as Milton's *Lycidas,* not to mention *Paradise Lost,* and the *tanka* is without question the true norm. Even as this fragmentation developed, however, there grew an opposite process of integration by which the *tanka* units were combined into larger wholes. Some of these larger wholes combine poems with prose, either by relating a poem to a real or imagined circumstance of composition or by making poems part of a flow of events, of plot. In the second of the imperial collections, the *Gosenshū* (951), for example, the compilers sometimes added long headnotes to the poems, giving them situations that were often fictional. As anyone who has read Japanese commentaries on poems will know, the belief that there must be some real situation behind the composition of a poem is a very enduring attitude, even while the thirst for actuality is often satisfied by what is transparently fictional. It is not a long step from poems with lengthy headnotes to "tales of poems" (*utamonogatari*), of which the most famous example is *The Tales of Ise,* based on poems by Narihira and on legends surrounding him. From that genre it is but another, though a longer, step to "fictional tales" (*tsukurimonogatari*), of which *The Tale of Genji* is the great exemplar. In this more extended form, prose unquestionably dominates verse, but the poems are highly important. They often give an imagistic coherence, as well as the title, to the books of *The Tale of Genji*; frequently poems in a later part echo poems in an earlier part; and numerous poetic motifs bearing on the meaning of the whole work run through this greatest of "fictional tales." To consider only gross numbers, what would a reviewer today make of a work of prose fiction like *The Tale of Genji,* with almost four thousand lines of poetry fully integrated into it? It is no criticism of *Dr. Zhivago* as a novel to say that, by comparison with *The Tale of Genji,* its cluster of poems at the end is awkward and poorly integrated.

Another mixed form is the poetic diary. The first of them, *The Tosa Diary* (ca. 935), which has fifty-nine poems, is about the length of an average short story. *The Pillow Book* (c. 1002) of Sei Shōnagon contains only thirty-seven poems in its considerable length, but *The Diary of Izumi Shikibu* includes over 140, better than three to a page on the average in a modern edition. Very little in Western literature prepares us for the naturalness with which prose and verse are combined in Japanese literature, from the early *Kojiki* to the *nō* and *kabuki* of much later times. Even after it is clear to us intellectually that we should not regard Japanese literary works in terms of our own genres, we may find it difficult emotionally to accept the fact that the same work may be called a tale (*monogatari*), a diary (*nikki*), or, significantly, a poetic collection (*kashū*). The shorter Japanese poetic units are quite simply more adhesive to fictional—or even nonfictional—strands of prose than our own discrete, autonomously conceived poems.

To a very considerable extent, then, a court poem is five lines in search of a context. But the context need not be made of prose. Collections such as the imperial anthologies show the same tendency to integration as do the diaries. The two main groups of poems in an imperial collection led the way to the practice of bringing separate poems together into a whole. The seasonal poems were arranged by a very natural temporal progression, in a sequence determined by the seasonal occurrence of natural events and the order of human responses to natural events set by the *Annual Ceremonial*. A temporal progression was also natural to the love poems, which were arranged in the pattern of a courtly love affair. In Japanese terms, such an arrangement is the most natural thing in the world, just as in Western terms, where poems and poets are thought of as discrete entities, it is natural to classify poems by the poet's name and chronologically by date of composition. The Japanese approach has one great advantage over ours: by integrating poems into a sequence of outer events without regard to authorship or date of composition, it so emphasizes their interrelationship as to create a new literary form. Anyone looking for a longish poem in Japanese need not despair: he can read through the 1,800 lines of love poetry in the *Kokinshū*. There he

will find what it is like to feel the first stirrings of love, to fall passionately in love with someone, to go through the whole course of
a courtly affair to its end in separation and sadness. Moreover, the
basic temporal progressions were in time augmented by spatial
progressions, and later by techniques of association that integrated
poems into a whole even when progression was infeasible. So if
our skeptical reader is in search of something still longer than the
love plot of the *Kokinshū*, he may sit down with the 9,875 lines of
the *Shinkokinshū*. If that does not slake his thirst, he may try the
13,935 lines of the *Gyokuyōshū*.

Most of us, however, will be satisfied by knowledge of the
principle and by acquaintance with an illustration of the practice
of integrating poems in a longer sequence. Among the winter
poems in the *Shinkokinshū* are thirteen (VI: 661–73) that are
part of a subsequence treating human affairs. These are in turn
part of a yet larger group of poems having snow as a central image.
We may look at the last four of these poems, which we come to in
the motif-sequence of winter, snow, and human affairs.

Poems

Was it not enough
To know loneliness without this?
—Along the hillslopes
The oak trees droop their leaves
And still the snow keeps falling.

Motifs

1. Speaker: observer
2. Time: daytime
3. Tone: loneliness
4. Place: hills; trees; snow

There is no shelter
Where I can rest my weary horse
And brush my laden sleeves:
The Sano ford and its adjoining fields
Spread over with a twilight in the snow.

1. Speaker: traveler
2. Time: evening
3. Tone: isolation
4. Place: river; outdoors, no
   shelter; snow

The path of him I long for
Across the foothills to where I wait
Must be wiped out:
The weight of snow grows greater
In the cedars standing at my eaves.

1. Speaker: woman await-
   ing lover
2. Time: evening
3. Tone: isolation
4. Place: indoors to shelter;
   trees; snow

Beneath the piling snow
The bamboos of Fushimi village
  Crack loudly in the night—
Even the path to love in dreams collapses
Into waking from the sounding snow.*

1. Speaker: woman dreaming of lover
2. Time: night
3. Tone: frustration
4. Place: indoors; bamboo from trees; snow

The temporal and spatial progressions and the development of imagery allow the reader to move smoothly from one poem to the next, enjoying the poems as integral parts of a larger poetic form. In what follows in this book, integration will be assumed as a characteristic feature of court poetry, although the poems will usually be considered outside their contexts.

It would be wrong to say that Japanese had ever really lost a feel for the way poems could be integrated by association and progression. The continuing popularity of the poetic diary in all such mutations as the travel record, and the way even independently composed *haiku* are grouped as variations on a theme, reveal that Japanese have treated their fragmented forms in ways that integrated them. But the detailed principles of integration through association and progression have been rediscovered only in recent years, in what must be considered one of the major literary discoveries, or recoveries, of our generation.

Another major way to "publish" poems was the poetry match (*utaawase*), which began as one of many kinds of matching: iris

* The poems run as follows:

Sabishisa o
Ika ni seyo tote
Okabe naru
Nara no ha shidari
Yuki no furu ran.
(670: *Fujiwara Kunifusa*)

Koma tomete
Sode uchiharau
Kage mo nashi
Sano no watari no
Yuki no yūgure.
(671: *Fujiwara Teika*)

Matsu hito no
Fumoto no michi wa
Taenu ran
Nokiba no sugi ni
Yuki omoru nari.
(672: *Fujiwara Teika*)

Yume kayou
Michi sae taenu
Kuretake no
Fushimi no sato no
Yuki no shitaore.
(673: *Fujiwara Ariie*)

roots might be compared, for example, or pictures.* The early matches were informal and intended apparently as pure entertainment, although given the Japanese reluctance to lose face there must have been some earnestness from the outset. Gradually poetry matches became more and more important, and as they did they became increasingly serious. When something of the spontaneity of the court was lost, poetry became a religious way of life (*michi*) by which one might hope for salvation. The formal rules by which the matches were conducted also became more serious. Over the two sides, Left and Right, were set judges who gave win, lose, and draw decisions, justifying their pronouncements with critical evaluations. It was even possible to appeal decisions. Records of many of the matches survive, many in minute detail, showing that after the early informal stages of development it became common to set topics in advance. Although the courtly tradition of the minnesingers and troubadours in the West was similar to that of the Japanese in providing a social context for poets and their songs, the practice of setting topics, like other devices of integration discussed above, is scarcely to be found in the West and can be considered characteristically Japanese.

Although the social context of poems in the poetry matches was not unlike the prose contexts in the tales and diaries, the poems written for the matches were integrated in more properly literary ways as well. In order to match the poems, common topics had to be given out to each side; and once a number of topics had been chosen, it was only natural that they should be fitted into a pattern. The readiest pattern was of course that of the imperial anthology. Sometimes the whole pattern of the anthology (suitably condensed) would be the basis for a contest, sometimes the pattern of a single section, such as the section on love. Perhaps the ultimate in integration of this kind is to be found in the "poetry matches with oneself" (*jikaawase*), in which the poet took two roles and played a kind of poetic chess with himself, sending the results to a distinguished judge for comment. The Priest Saigyō (1118–90) was one of those who vied with himself in this fashion, notably in

---

* A chapter of *The Tale of Genji* (Waley trans., II, viii) is devoted to "The Picture Competition."

his *Poetry Contest at the Mimosuso River* (*Mimosusogawa Uta-awase*), in which he pitted the Visitor to the Mountain Hut against the Master of the Path Across the Moors. When he had completed this sequence, he sent it off to his friend Shunzei, who was the best judge as well as one of the greatest poets of the day.

Such conventions of integration reached their ideal or characteristic form in the poetic sequence of this or that number of poems, commonly one hundred (*hyakushuuta*). Again a form modeled on the imperial collections, the sequence was based on such topics as the spirit of departing spring, the autumn wind, secret love, or meeting with a lover who will not love. Like the imperial collections, the sequences came to be ordered not only according to the major embracing pattern, and not only by techniques of temporal progression, but also by local spatial progressions and associations of situation, rhetoric, and imagery. In effect, the usual hundred-poem sequence amounts to a single work of five hundred lines. This work is made up of elements that may or may not be as tightly woven together as the sections of a long Western poem—some sequences are relatively loosely put together, others are astonishingly integrated. Whether closely or loosely integrated, however, the hundred-poem sequence is what may be called the standard private form of later court poetry, just as the imperial collection is the standard public form.

Such forms and conventions of Japanese court poetry are so highly wrought that they raise again the relation, or tension, between Japanese faith in spontaneous emotion and Japanese prizing of artistic conventions. If a person is asked to compose a poem on "Snow at a Mountain Village" on a balmy spring day in the capital, then he, and we, might well ask what has happened to Tsurayuki's conception of men and women being naturally given to song. Yet Tsurayuki himself—in his own practice, in the famous Preface, and in his brilliantly conceived organization of the *Kokinshū*—was instrumental in establishing court poetry as an art. He confirmed the importance of techniques and subjects adapted from Chinese poetry of the Six Dynasties (A.D. 222–589). He helped set the form of the imperial collections. He distinguished between informal poetry of the kind found in *The Tosa Diary*

32

and the formal poetry required for social occasions. Of course, he did not establish the canons of court poetry by himself, but he is a convenient symbol for a generation that made court poetry an established art. What looks at first glance, then, like a dilemma in court poetry—the tension between feeling and convention—can be a force for poetic creation. In the generations after Tsurayuki, the tension between natural feeling and courtly art became even stronger as the informal poetic subjects of Tsurayuki's day became set topics (*dai*) for formal occasions like poetry matches. What is involved is a special version of one of the oldest and most persistent problems of art—its relation to, and formal freedom from, life.

The creative tension between art and spontaneous feeling was reconciled earlier in practice than in theory. We can infer from Tsurayuki's practice his unspoken rule: Write about what moves you, but write with all the art at your command. Only the naïve or the cynical doubt that simplicity is an art and that art may possess immediacy of feeling. Tsurayuki's *Tosa Diary* shows that he took a natural way in dealing with an artistic problem. Among the characters who compose poems on the voyage home are a woman (the fictional diarist) who has lost her child, children, a seasick old woman, and a wonderful provincial bumpkin who fancies himself the local laureate. Each of these composes poems requiring a style either simple or intensely individual if his poems are to carry conviction. Yet the art of simplicity and sincerity remains an art, and we should have no cause for surprise that a mark of one of the kinds of Japanese classicism is the same as for one of the Western kinds—simplicity.

Shunzei gives us another kind of insight. By his generation (he was born in 1114), almost all serious poetry was composed for specific occasions or on set topics. But that did not mean that there was any less emotion behind his poems than behind those of earlier poets. Nor was he inconsistent with his principles in his late years —and he lived to be 90—in composing a poem in which the speaker was a young woman in love, because the truth of her feeling was a truth he shared. If that were not the case, we readers would also have no business reading poetry. Certainly Shunzei showed in his

33

actions how deeply poetry moved him. The poet Shinkei (1406–75) gives us this picture of Shunzei composing poetry on a winter's night.

> Very late at night he would sit by his bed in front of an oil lamp so dim that it was difficult to tell whether it was burning or not, and with a tattered court robe thrown over his shoulders and an old court cap pulled down to his ears, he would lean on an armrest, hugging a wooden brazier for warmth, while he recited verse to himself in an undertone. Deep into the night, when everyone else was asleep, he would sit there bent over, weeping softly.*

The tension between art and life is one that we implicitly understand to be reconciled by the poet as he creates, like Shunzei here, or the reader as he responds.

The Japanese saw this inevitable tension in terms of the distinction we have made earlier, between *kotoba,* "words," and *kokoro,* "heart." The words had to supply the most refined, the most artistic medium possible, but the "heart" needed to remain free. Teika, Shunzei's son and the greatest poet of his age, wrote of the matter in his *Fundamentals of Poetic Composition (Eiga Taigai).*

> In the expression of the emotions originality merits the first consideration. (That is, one should look for sentiments unsung by others and sing them.) The words used, however, should be old ones. (The vocabulary should be restricted to words used by the masters of the Three Anthologies: the same words are proper for all poets, whether ancient or modern.)†

Kotoba, as we have seen, means more than just language; it involves the materials shaped into poetry. Similarly, *kokoro,* the shaping spirit, implies more than just new ideas or feelings; it involves all that makes a poem live. Shunzei and Teika espoused

---

* *Sasamegoto, NKGT,* V, 268.

† *Eiga Taigai,* translated in *Sources of the Japanese Tradition,* compiled by Ryusaku Tsunoda, *et al.* (New York, 1958), pp. 183–84. The "Three Anthologies" *(Sandaishū)* are the first three imperial collections, *Kokinshū, Gosenshū,* and *Shūishū.*

a shorter version of Teika's remarks, and the briefer phrases suggest the formulation of the tension between art and feeling throughout most of court poetry. Their motto was "old words, new heart" (*kotoba furuku, kokoro atarashi*). The *kotoba* from which poetry is made seemed to have been discovered for all time by the generation of Tsurayuki, but the *kokoro* of poetry perforce changed with changing experience. Such an attitude is in sharp contrast to Wordsworth's insistence in his Preface to *Lyrical Ballads* that the poet reject traditional poetic language. But it was a Japanese decision for Japanese poets.

Very possibly one reason why the spontaneous expression of feeling is extolled by Japanese from Tsurayuki in A.D. 905 to Ishikawa Takuboku in this century is that Japanese society has so long been hedged about by restrictions that stifle individual spontaneity. The principle behind this interpretation is that one prizes what one does not have enough of. On the other hand, it is also possible to look upon typical Japanese experience as so very individual, emotional, and even anarchic that the most artistic and conventional forms were necessary to give such experience meaningful shape. The principle behind this interpretation is that a civilization finds what it needs to retain its self-control. It goes without saying that, because they are human, Japanese have never been wholly able to realize their ideals of art as well as life, of "words" as well as "heart," of forms and conventions as well as spontaneous feeling. For all that, we who study Japanese poetry have an obligation to understand its old words, and we shall be wasting our time if we cannot find a spontaneous and natural impulse to affirmation, like that Tsurayuki attributed to the warbler among the blossoms and the frog in its fresh waters. We should also discover at the same time depths of suffering conveyed by poetry. The fact that Shunzei could be said to weep as he composed or recited poetry late at night shows that the most sophisticated court poet could respond to the darker human truths embodied in his art.

35

CHAPTER THREE

Hitomaro

The century of poetry from 686 to 784, sometimes designated as the early literary period,* is one of the most vigorous periods of Japanese history. Following the Taika Reform of 645, it is the time of the establishment of the first "permanent" capital at Nara, a time of remarkable achievement in politics as well as sculpture, in religion as well as architecture. Much of this achievement was due to the examples of China and Korea which Japanese held before themselves. In 602, for instance, when a Korean priest called Kwallŭk came with books as tribute to the Japanese court, he was promptly appointed teacher to various courtiers.

> Ōchin, the ancestor of the scribes of Yako, studied the art of calendar making. Kōsō, Ōtomo no Suguri, studied astronomy and the art of invisibility. Hinamitatsu, the Imperial Chieftain of Yamashiro, studied magic. They all studied so far as to perfect themselves in these arts.†

But much of the achievement was due also to the development at this time of pride in things distinctly Japanese. The society was at once stable and alive with change. It is an age of which we can expect great things, and no one who has seen its temples or read its poetry can fail to be impressed.

One collection, the *Man'yōshū*, contains almost all the surviving poetry of the period—about 4,500 poems, mostly *tanka* and *chōka*. Although our knowledge of the date of compilation and the com-

---

* For the logic behind the periodization used in this book, see *Japanese Court Poetry*, p. viii. In general, although the names for them are different, the periods themselves are those distinguished by Japanese scholars.

† Quoted from Ryusaku Tsunoda, *et al.*, eds., *Sources of the Japanese Tradition* (New York, 1958), p. 95; taken from *Nihongi*, trans. Aston, II, 126.

pilers of this anthology is sketchy, we do know that one of the
compilers, and presumably the last, was Ōtomo Yakamochi (718–
85), not an invisible Ōtomo like Suguri, and himself a major poet.
Various now lost collections are referred to in notes, suggesting
that the *Man'yōshū* is an anthology of anthologies, and there is
clear enough evidence to show that Yakamochi was an antiquarian or literary anthropologist who sought out provincial poems.
Whether from such an antiquarian impulse or some other, the
compilers chose earlier poems as well as those of their contemporaries, thereby producing a collection that resembled in hetero-
geneity those compiled in later centuries at imperial command.
The earliest person mentioned is Empress Iwa, who died about
A.D. 347 innocent of the poem attributed to her; and the last dat-
able poem is from 759. Unquestionably the greatest poet represented in the *Man'yōshū* is Kakinomoto Hitomaro (fl. ca. 680–
700).

Japanese scholars believe that it is possible to follow the development of Japanese poetry from primitive times to Hitomaro's day
by evidence of poems which, though not ordered chronologically
in the *Man'yōshū,* may be set in a theoretical pattern of develop-
ing art. The irregular prosody of the very first poem, for example,
suggests its origins in primitive song, while its relatively sophisticated syntactic parallelism suggests a date of composition in the
early literary period. The anthology attributes the poem to Emperor Yūryaku (?418–?479), but the situation is so obviously fictional that we can only assume it to have been written at an unknown date by an unknown hand for a Yamato chieftain, who is
pictured as a young man improving his time with an attractive
girl he chances upon.

Ko mo yo	With a basket
Miko mochi	A pretty basket,
Fukushi mo yo	With a trowel,
Mibukushi mochi	A pretty trowel in your hand,
Kono oka ni	O young maid gathering
Na tsumasu ko	Greens on this hill,
Ie kikana	Tell me your home,
Norasane	Tell about yourself.
Sora mitsu	I hold the power

Yamato no kuni wa	Over this land of Yamato
Oshinabete	Broad under heaven,
Ware koso ore	And I am a chief known to all;
Shikinabete	Famous everywhere,
Ware koso mase	My power is known to all.
Ware ni koso wa	And so to no one else,
Norame	Yes, to me alone,
Ie o mo na o mo.	Tell of your home and your name.

Such early poems have their charm, but they are far removed from the achievement of Hitomaro. Considerable steps toward poetic maturity were taken during the reign of Emperor Tenji (626–71), who seems genuinely to have written the poems attributed to him and who, in any event, reigned over a literary-minded court that had an attentive eye cocked on China. Princess Nukata (fl. ca. 660–90), for example, introduced the sophisticated debate (which still can excite polite disagreement in Japan) whether spring or autumn is the lovelier season. Her poem "On Preferring the Autumn Hills" (*MYS*, I: 16) is regular in prosody and, apart from ending with a triplet, forms what can be described as a prosodically perfect *chōka*.

Fuyugomori	When spring at last
Haru sarikureba	Is freed from winter's bonds,
Nakazarishi	The silent birds
Tori mo kinakinu	Arrive in their full song
Sakazarishi	And lifeless flowers
Hana mo sakeredo	Burst forth in brilliant bloom;
Yama o shigemi	Yet I cannot find
Irite mo torazu	The flowers on their luxuriant slopes
Kusa fukami	Or appreciate the blossoms
Torite mo mizu	Hopelessly entangled in the grass.
Akiyama no	However, when I see
Ko no ha o mite wa	The leaves upon the autumn hills,
Momiji o ba	My eager hands
Torite zo shinobu	Tremble with their load of crimson leaves
Aoki o ba	And with reluctance
Okite zo nageku	Leave the green ones on their boughs—
Soko shi urameshi	Yes, the green ones are the pity,
Akiyama ware wa.	And the autumn hills for me.

It is a pleasant, if not a great, poem. The absence of one or more envoys in the *tanka* form is not extraordinary, but the fact may suggest that the *chōka*-envoy form developed after Princess Nukata's time; we may also speculate, with Japanese scholars, that the envoy grew from the example of Chinese poets, some of whom added to their long ornate compositions (*fu*) a short concluding poem (*tz'u* or *fan tz'u,* "repeating words"). Whatever the origins of the *tanka* envoy, it seems clear that most of the formal conventions of court poetry took shape in the reign of Emperor Tenji.

The maturation of forms and themes gives promise of greater things. Native resources had been directed artistically by such borrowed techniques as complex parallelisms and by a corresponding sophistication of subject and theme. The desire to emulate continental culture was accompanied by pride in a Japanese civilization burgeoning with numerous fruits of civilized activity. Out of this time of development and possibility emerged Hitomaro, whose poems are among the greatest in the language. Although much about him is obscure, we know that he was a courtier of middling rank. He was sent by the court to such remote places as Iwami and recalled thence to the capital; this we infer from two poems entitled "On Parting from His Wife as He Set Out from Iwami for the Capital" (*MYS,* II: 131–33, 135–37). Given the complex marriage customs of that day, it is not absolutely certain, though it is of course likely, that the wife is the same person in each poem of departure. It is almost certain, on the other hand, that she, or they, is not the same person as the woman or women mourned in the two poems written "After the Death of His Wife" (*MYS,* II: 207–9, 210–12), since these poems are set near Nara, not Iwami. To complicate matters further, there is a named wife, Yosami, who mourned his death (*MYS,* II: 224–25). Hitomaro wrote about himself and those close to him, about the deaths of the great as well as the humble, about those at court and those away. He wrote of the ruined capital of Ōmi and of the rocky seacoast of Iwami. What gives his poems their particular atmosphere, whatever their subject, is his interest both in man as an individual and in man benignly but firmly caught up in a larger scheme of things.

One of the most striking things about Hitomaro's poems is that they are commonly public in mode. It is not just that some of them concern public events and historical matters; it is that he stresses the things men share rather than the things that distinguish one man from another in their private lives. Serious court poetry subsequent to the *Man'yōshū* may well be called formal and social, but it is not public. For this characteristic alone, the early literary period claims a special place in the history of court poetry.

One of the topics common to public poetry of numerous traditions is the death of princes and other exalted figures, and Hitomaro tried his hand at the subject a number of times. Although common, the topic is not an easy one to treat meaningfully. It requires that the death be made of public importance, that a true worth or achievement in the dead be established, and that the speaker be involved in the loss. The longest poem in the *Man'yōshū*, Hitomaro's "On the Lying-in-State of Prince Takechi" (*MYS*, II: 199–201), shows one way of measuring up to the requirements. Takechi, son of Emperor Temmu, was commander-in-chief in the War of Jinshin (672), and both prime minister and crown prince under his mother, the Empress Jitō. He died in 696 before he could succeed to the throne. The poem is unique among court poems in describing a battle.

Kakemaku mo	To think of it	
Yuyushiki ka mo	Fills my soul with a holy fear,	
Iwamaku mo	And to speak of it	
Aya ni kashikoki	Makes my voice quiver with dread:	
Asuka no	Our sovereign Lord	5
Makami no hara ni	Who ruled over all the land in peace,	
Hisakata no	Who with royal wisdom	
Amatsumikado o	In a manner befitting his godliness,	
Kashikoku mo	Appointed in the past	
Sadametamaite	The site for his august palace,	10
Kamusabu to	Lofty as the heavens,	
Iwagakurimasu	Upon the divine plain of Makami	
Yasumishishi	In the land of Asuka,	
Wago ōkimi no	Vanishing within its rock-bound walls—	
Kikoshimesu	Yes, that very sovereign	15
Sotomo no kuni no	Once crossed the pine-clad crest of Fuwa	
Maki tatsu	Far off to the north	
Fuwayama koete	In the vast domain beneath his sway,	
Komatsurugi	Vouchsafing to descend	

Wazamigahara no	Upon the hill-ringed plain of Wazami— ²⁰
Karimiya ni	Ringed like a Korean sword.
Amoriimashite	For a time he set his palace in the fields,
Ame no shita	Where, with divine intent
Osametamai	To bring stability to the world
Osu kuni o	And order to his realm, ²⁵
Sadametamau to	He summoned to his imperial side
Tori ga naku	Bold warriors from the East,
Azuma no kuni no	Where the speech of men sounds as strange
Miikusa o	As the crowing of cocks,
Meshitamaite	And saying, "Let the belligerence ³⁰
	of the people
Chihayaburu	Now be pacified,
Hito o yawase to	And let the rebelliousness of the provinces
Matsurowanu	Swiftly be put down,"
Kuni o osame to	He bestowed command over all his men
Miko nagara	Upon our noble Prince, ³⁵
Maketamaeba	To carry out the royal will.
Ōmimi ni	So it was our Prince
Tachi toriobashi	Quickly buckled to his waist
Ōmite ni	His great long sword,
Yumi torimotashi	Seized his war bow in his hand, ⁴⁰
Miikusa o	And with fierce battle cry
Adomoitamai	Urged on the valiant fighting men.
Totonouru	Through his serried ranks
Tsuzumi no oto wa	The booming of the war drums echoed
Ikazuchi no	Like crashing thunder; ⁴⁵
Oto to kiku made	To the enemies' affrighted ears
Fukinaseru	The awful music
Kuda no oto mo	Of battle horns blown with fierce resolve
Atamitaru	Seemed like the roaring
Tora ka hoyuru to	Of tigers as they spring upon their prey; ⁵⁰
Morobito no	Their stoutest men
Obiyuru made ni	Trembled in terror at the alarm.
Sasagetaru	Fluttering in the wind,
Hata no nabiki wa	The banners that our Prince had raised
Fuyugomori	Looked like the hungry flames ⁵⁵
Haru sarikureba	Of the fires they kindle on all the fields
Nogoto ni	In the early spring
Tsukite aru hi no	To burn away the grasses withered
Kaze no muta	By the winter's cold.

Nabiku ga gotoku
　Torimotaru
Yuhazu no sawaki
　Miyuki furu
Fuyu no hayashi ni
　Tsumuji ka mo
Imakiwataru to
　Omou made
Kiki no kashikoku
　Hikihanatsu
Ya no shigekeku
　Ōyuki no
Midarete kitare
　Matsurowazu
Tachimukaishi mo
　Tsuyu shimo no
Kenaba kenubeku
　Yuku tori no
Arasou hashi ni
　Watarai no
Itsuki no miya yu
　Kamukaze ni
Ifukimatowashi
　Amakumo o
Hi no me mo misezu
　Tokoyami ni
Ōitamaite
　Sadameteshi
Mizuho no kuni o
　Kamu nagara
Futoshikimashite
　Yasumishishi
Wago ōkimi no
　Ame no shita
Mōshitamaeba

Yorozuyo ni
Shika shi mo aran to
Yūhana no
Sakayuru toki ni
Wago ōkimi

His warriors aimed their great war bows: 60
　A myriad bowstrings
All released as one upon the air
　Was frightful to the ears;
The sound was like a violent whirlwind
　Rushing through the trees 65
Of some forest in the grip of winter,
　Whose savage blizzards
Fill all the air with blinding snow—
　Yes, like a great blizzard
Came the swirling cloud of arrows 70
　That burst upon them,
Driven like snow before the wind.
　The armies clashed,
For even the enemies of our Prince,
　Rebels that they were, 75
Knowing they must perish like dew or frost
　Fading beneath the sun,
Took courage in their desperation,
　Each striving to be first
Like birds that vie upon the wing— 80
　When, lo, from Itsuki,
From the Great Shrine in holy Watarai,
　A divine wind sprang up,
Blowing confusion upon the enemy,
　Bearing heavenly clouds 85
To blacken the sacred sun's bright form,
　Covering the earth
With an impenetrable darkness:
　Thus did our great Prince
Bring peace to this rice-abounding land, 90
　And while a very goddess
Reigned in splendor from her throne,
　He graciously undertook
To govern the earth on her behalf.

So the land prospered, 95
Like flowers of the mulberry tree,
　And all men thought
It would flourish for a thousand ages,
　When suddenly

Miko no mikado o	The palace of our noble Prince	100
Kamumiya ni	Became a shrine	
Yosoimatsurite	Entombing his divine remains.	
Tsukawashishi	Now the courtiers	
Mikado no hito mo	Who waited on our Lord in life	
Shirotae no	Were robed in hempen white,	105
Asagoromo ki	Yes, clothed in the white hemp of	
	mourning,	
Haniyasu no	And day by day	
Mikado no hara ni	Beneath the madder-colored sun	
Akane sasu	They crept about,	
Hi no kotogoto	Falling to the ground like stricken deer	110
Shishijimono	Upon the fields	
Ihaifushitsutsu	Before his palace gate at Haniyasu,	
Nubatama no	And when the night	
Yūbe ni nareba	Grew to darkness like a bead of jet,	
Ōtono o	They crawled away,	115
Furisakemitsutsu	Bowing in grief to the ground like quails	
Uzura nasu	And glancing back	
Ihaimotohori	Toward the great palace of their Lord.	
Samoraedo	Though they would serve him,	
Samoraieneba	He was no longer theirs to serve;	120
Harutori no	They could only raise	
Samayoinureba	Weak-throated cries like birds in spring.	
Nageki mo	And before their grief	
Imada suginu ni	Had even begun to pass away,	
Omoi mo	Before their longing	125
Imada tsukineba	Had lost its first shocked anguish,	
Koto saeku	He was borne away	
Kudara no hara yu	In holy procession across the fields	
Kamuhaburi	Of Kudara, whose very name	
Haburiimashite	Sounds remote as the speech of	130
	far Cathay;	
	He was laid to rest	
Asamo yoshi	Forever in the sacred shrine	
Kinoe no miya o	Of lofty Kinoe,	
Tokomiya to	Pure as cloth of the whitest hemp,	
Takaku matsurite	A veritable god	135
Kamu nagara	Enshrined forever in those sacred halls.	
Shizumarimashinu	But though our Prince,	
Shikaredo mo	Our royal master, is taken from us,	
Wago ōkimi no	There still remains	
Yorozuyo to		

	140
Omohoshimeshite	On the Holy Hill of Kagu his great palace
Tsukurashishi	That he erected,
Kaguyama no miya	Intending that it should endure
Yorozuyo ni	Ten thousand ages—
Sugin to omoe ya	Yes, though ten thousand ages pass away 145
Ame no goto	It will endure,
Furisakemitsutsu	And we shall gaze up at its eminence
Tamatasuki	As to the heavens,
Kakete shinowan	In longing for our royal master
Kashikokaredo mo.	Though holy dread may fill our hearts.

Envoys

Hisakata no	Although our Lord
Ame shirashinuru	Now reigns in splendor from his shrine
Kimi yue ni	As a god on high,
Hitsuki mo shirazu	Our yearning for him knows no changing
Koiwataru ka mo.	With the passing of the days and months.

Haniyasu no	Just as the waters
Ike no tsutsumi no	Pent up by walls in Haniyasu Pool
Komorinu no	Do not know where to flow,
Yukue o shirani	So now the courtiers of the Prince
Toneri wa matou.	Are trapped with no direction to their lives.

The long middle section of the poem, lines 37–94, deals with the prince's great battle, creating a sense of urgency and of momentous, even miraculous, events. The death of such a hero, treated in lines 95–136, is felt as a grievous loss because he had brought peace. We are convinced of the loss. But what of Hitomaro himself? At the very beginning (1–4) and very end (149) of the *chōka,* he presents himself as one almost frightened by what has happened. In the envoys, he suggests that, like the other courtiers, he has lost direction in his life. But matters are not quite so simple, because, although his grief is sincere, it is also uncommonly self-possessed and knowing. The prince is mourned for the fact that he "Graciously undertook / To govern the earth on [his mother's] behalf" (93–94). But his role as prime minister is merely touched upon in that pair of lines. Instead, two rather different matters are stressed. The most important thing to emerge is the society, the nation, with its men of various ranks. At the beginning of the poem the prince responds to the commands of the emperor his father; at the end the prince's courtiers show their allegiance. Although tightly woven into the whole, two lines (89–90)—"Thus did our great Prince / Bring peace to this rice-abounding land"—suggest that the land and its prosperity are central concerns of the poem, and that these concerns are dependent on a ruler with sons to serve his ends, just as courtiers are dependent on princes.

Hitomaro's second major concern is with the prince's achievement—winning the war. It is typical of the warm and kindly irony we find throughout Hitomaro's poems that war should be necessary for peace and that the prince's efforts should be successful only by virtue of the miracle of an eclipse. The growth of peace from war is an ancient human hope, and the sanction of the supernatural is of course a common sign of special favor from heaven to the hero. Yet there is more to it than that—the prince's enemies are treated with respect and humanity and, whatever the prince's divine attributes, he is dead. That is one aspect of the irony so distinctive in Hitomaro's poems. Another is the fact that the prince's palace outlasts the man who made it. As always, however, the ironies are redeemed. The prince is dead but sincerely mourned. His palace lasts after him but reminds men of him.

Yet more importantly, the emphasis upon natural continuity and order (which is the obvious function of the first thirty-six lines and which emerges by implication later in the stress upon ceremony and divinity) is one that brings consolation. Finally, there is the loss of the possibility of extraordinary action, the loss of inspired leadership, which leaves the courtiers frustrated—dammed up like the waters of the stone-banked pool. We see that in the end it is the order of the state that sustains the tragedy more than the prince himself.

Another poem, "On Passing the Ruined Capital of Ōmi" (*MYS,* I: 29–31), purports to give Hitomaro's reactions to the ruins of the court that had been moved to Ōmi in 667 only to be destroyed in the War of Jinshin in 672 which was executed so well by Prince Takechi. It begins with a reference to "the first age" of Emperor Jimmu, the legendary first sovereign of Japan, and refers in lines 23–27 to Emperor Tenji.

Tamatasuki	It was Mount Unebi,
Unebi no yama no	Fair as a maiden gird with lovely scarf,
Kashihara no	Where from the first age
Hijiri no miyo yu	Of our sun-sovereigns there rose up
Aremashishi	Kashihara Palace; 5
Kami no kotogoto	And there each of our divinities
Tsuga no ki no	Ruled in a line unbroken
Iya tsugitsugi ni	Like a column of many evergreens,
Ame no shita	Beginning their sway
Shirashimeshishi o	Of this nation under the heavens 10
Sora ni mitsu	In Yamato province,
Yamato o okite	Which adds its brightness to the sky.

Aoni yoshi	What purpose was there
Narayama o koe	To leave it, to cross the hills of Nara,
Ikasama ni	Rich in colored earth, 15
Omohoshimese ka	To establish a new capital in a land
Amazakaru	Beyond the horizon,
Hina ni wa aredo	To choose a palace site off in the country?
Iwabashiru	But it was in Ōmi province,
Ōmi no kuni no	Where the water rushes over rocks, 20
Sasanami no	In Sasanami
Ōtsu no miya ni	At this lofty Ōtsu palace,
Ame no shita	Where our ruler
Shirashimeshiken	Began his rule over all our nation;
Sumeroki no	Here beneath the heavens 25
Kami no mikoto no	Yes, here it was our sovereign lord
Ōmiya wa	Made his imperial court.

Koko to kikedo mo	Though men relate how at this site
Ōtono wa	There rose a palace,
Koko to iedo mo	Though they insist high halls 30
	stood here,
Harukusa no	Now wild grasses grow
Shigeku oitaru	In a springtime of profusion
Kasumi tachi	And haze-streamers float
Haruhi no kireru	Across the mild spring sun, misting over
Momoshiki no	The ruins of a palace 35
Ōmiyadokoro	Built on foundations multi-walled,
Mireba kanashi mo.	And just to look upon it makes me sad.

46

Envoys

Sasanami no	The Cape of Kara
Shiga no Karasaki	At Shiga in Sasanami still remains
Sakiku aredo	As it ever was,
Ōmiyabito no	But though it wait throughout the ages,
Fune machikanetsu.	The courtiers' pleasure boats will
	not return.

Sasanami no	Although the waters
Shiga no ōwada	Off the Shiga coast in Sasanami
Yodomu to mo	Stand still and wait,
Mukashi no hito ni	Never again can they hope to greet
Mata mo awame	The men now vanished in the past.
ya mo.	

In this *chōka*, too, there is a strong sense of the continuity of the state from the first to the most recent of emperors, and here, too, a sense of loss cuts across the celebration of that continuity. Once again the *chōka* begins with movement and achievement and ends with a sorrowing speaker. The first envoy achieves a perfect tone of grief in its regret and frustration, indeed its desolation, yet also in its celebration of all that once was. And in the second envoy, we find once more the gentle irony of which Hitomaro is so fond. The envoys tell of the loss suffered by the Cape of Kara and the waters of Lake Biwa—both will sorely miss the men whose very capital is now overgrown with weeds. Yet it is the men rather than the cape or the lake who have lost life, society, civilization—all. We are made aware of the tragedy in this gentle manner so that we may share the broad view in which Hitomaro encloses his sense of loss. By transferring the human tragedy to nature and to history he has permitted the ironic difference between the real loss and that which is talked about to be a consolation for the double loss.

One of Hitomaro's most appealing poems is "On Seeing the Body of a Man Lying among the Stones on the Island of Samine in Sanuki Province" (*MYS*, II: 220-22). It is a strange topic, but Japanese scholars are now agreed that the poem describes the results of a typhoon on the Inland Sea. In view of Japanese fears of ritual defilement by contact with the dead, it has been suggested that the poem is a form of exorcism; the use of the polite second-person noun for the dead man is among the evidence offered in support of this hypothesis. Whatever the actual circumstances, the poem is remarkable for its balance between identification of the speaker with the dead man and ironic separation from him.

Tamamo yoshi	O the precious land of Sanuki,
Sanuki no kuni wa	Resting where the seaweed glows like gems!
Kunikara ka	Perhaps for its precious nature
Miredo mo akanu	I never tire in my gazing on it,
Kamukara ka	Perhaps for its holy name
Kokoda tōtoki	It is the most divine of sights.
Ametsuchi	It will flourish and endure
Hitsuki to tomo ni	Together with the heavens and earth,
Tariyukan	With the shining sun and moon,
Kami no miomo to	For through successive ages it has come down
Tsugite kuru	That the landface is the face of a god.
Naka no minato yu	Having rushed our ship upon the breakers
Fune ukete	From the port of Naka,
Waga kogikureba	We came rowing steadily until the wind
Tokitsukaze	That rises with the tides
Kumoi ni fuku ni	Stormed down from the dwelling of the clouds—
Oki mireba	Looking back upon the open sea
Toinami tachi	I saw waves gather in their mounting surges,
He mireba	And looking off beyond the prow
Shiranami sawaku	I saw the white waves dashing on the surf.
Isanatori	In awe of the terrible sea,
Umi o kashikomi	Where whales are hunted down as prey,
Yuku fune no	We clutched the steering oar,
Kaji hikiorite	Straining the plunging ship upon its course;
Ochikochi no	And though here and there
Shima wa ōkedo	We saw the scattered island coasts

5

10

15

20

25

Nakuwashi	To dash upon for safety,
Samine no shima no	We sought haven on rugged Samine,
Arisomo ni	The isle so beautiful in name.
Iorite mireba	Erecting a little shelter, we looked about, 30
Nami no to no	And then we saw you:
Shigeki hamabe o	Pillowed upon your shaking beach,
Shikitae no	Using those wave-beaten rocks
Makura ni nashite	As if the coast were spread out for your bedding;
Aradoko ni	On such a rugged place 35
Korofusu kimi ga	You have laid yourself to rest.
Ie shiraba	If I but knew your home,
Yukite mo tsugen	I would go tell them where you sleep;
Tsuma shiraba	If your wife but knew this place,
Ki mo towamashi o	She would come here searching for you, 40
Tamahoko no	But knowing nothing of the way—
Michi dani shirazu	The way straight as a jeweled spear—
Oboboshiku	How must she be waiting,
Machi ka kou ran	How anxiously now longing for you,
Hashiki tsumara wa.	She so dear who was your wife. 45

Envoys

Tsuma mo araba	If your wife were here,
Tsumite tagemashi	She would be out gathering your food,
Sami no yama	She would pick the greens
No no e no uhagi	From the hill slopes of Samine—
Suginikerazu ya.	But is their season not now past?
Okitsunami	So you rest your head,
Kiyoru ariso o	Pillowed on the rocky spread-out bedding
Shikitae no	Of this rugged shore,
Makura to makite	While the furious, wind-driven surf
Naseru kimi ka mo.	Pounds ever in from off the sea.

The middle section of the *chōka*, lines 12–36, brings together the narrator and the dead man by describing the storm encountered by them both. They share the storm, the coast of Samine, and the hazards of travel. The dead man is addressed as if he were alive, his posture seen as if he were lying asleep. The last section of the *chōka* introduces the narrator's concern for the dead man's wife—

it is typical of Hitomaro to assume that he has a loving wife—and introduces as well the theme of man's ignorance in the world. The wife does not even know her husband is dead, let alone where his body lies, and the narrator is helpless to tell her.

The first envoy suggests, with Hitomaro's customary gentle irony, that if the wife were present, she would want to gather greens—but unfortunately their season is past. The irony insists that it is a man's life that is past, but the insistence carries with it a yet greater sympathy which renders the irony into a species of human tact akin to love. The second envoy leaves us with an image of the human condition: man pillowed, in death, on a rocky coast where the storm-beaten surf crashes in. There the poem ends. It is not strange that during World War II Japanese found the poem a moving clarification of the tragedy they endured. It was the more moving because the desolate conclusion is but one part of the greater scheme of things.

The first part of the poem, lines 1-11, is an overture, a device that Hitomaro liked and established as a convention of the *chōka*. It resembles similar openings in Pindar's or in Dryden's odes. In such a splendid evocation of awe and wonder for the land, we see the obvious contribution of Shinto animism. Some scholars think that Hitomaro designed overtures like this on the pattern of the Shinto liturgies (*norito*). But the date when *norito* were written is obscure, and it may be that the influence was the other way around. What is certain is that the opening lines give us the kind of celebration of land and life that Japanese owe to Shinto, and that these lines are closely related to Hitomaro's purpose in the rest of the poem. Partly the connection is ironic: Samine is "The isle so beautiful in name"—and so deadly in effect. Yet the irony is finally reconciled by Hitomaro's suggestion of the holiness of the land and the continuity of time. If one must die, and one must, then divine Sanuki province, and in it Samine of the lovely name, is a good place to die. The reconciliation by no means cancels the irony or overcomes the terrible deprivation. After all, the order of the poem gives us first the consolation and then the tragedy, rather than the reverse, which would be more consoling. And yet the overture makes the tragedy bearable. It assuages human suffering by showing that man participates, however inscrutably, in a divine order.

According to T. S. Eliot, the one essential quality in works and authors that we term "classic" is maturity. Hitomaro possesses a rare maturity, a wisdom enabling him to examine all the facts of the situation, to understand their terrible significance, to evaluate them, and to keep his composure. Another characteristic of Hitomaro as a poet is his essential normality. He sees the dead man and thinks at once of his wife and the domestic scene of preparing a meal. If it be thought remarkable that such of Hitomaro's ironies as this are comforting, and it is, the reason is to be found in the warm, understanding, and normal humanity that we still feel some thirteen centuries after this obscure courtier was born.

Hitomaro was also a personal, if not precisely a private, poet. He wrote of his own affairs, always establishing their ordinary humanity and their connection with familiar places and processes that could be shared by all who knew his poems. One such personal poem is the second he wrote "On Parting from His Wife as He Set Out from Iwami for the Capital" (*MYS*, II: 135–37).

Tsuno sahau	It was by the sea of Iwami
Iwami no umi no	Where the clinging ivy creeps across the rocks,
Koto saeku	By the waters off Cape Kara,
Kara no saki naru	A land remote as the speech of far Cathay—
Ikuri ni zo	Yes, there where the seaweed grows, 5
Fukamiru ouru	Clinging to rocks fathoms beneath the waves,
Ariso ni zo	And where on the stony strand
Tamamo wa ouru	The seaweed glows like polished gems.
Tamamo nasu	My young wife dwells there,
Nabikineshi ko o	Who like seaweed bent to the 10 current of love,
Fukamiru no	The girl who slept beside me
Fukamete moedo	Soft and lithesome as the gem-like water plants.
Saneshi yo wa	Now those nights seem few
Ikuda mo arazu	When we held each other close in sleep.

51

Hau tsuta no
Wakare shi kureba
Kimo mukau
Kokoro o itami
Omoitsutsu
Kaerimi suredo

We parted unwillingly,   15
Clinging to each other like ivy creepers;
  My heart ached and swelled
Against the ribs that would hold it,
  And when my yearning drew me
To pause, look back, and see her   20
  once again

Ōfune no
Watari no yama no
Momijiba no
Chiri no magai ni
Imo ga sode
Saya ni mo miezu

Waving her sleeves in farewell,
They were already taken from my sight,
  Hidden by the leaves
Falling like a curtain in their yellow whirl
  At the crest of Mount Watari,   25
A crest like a wave's that bears a
  ship away.

Tsumagomoru
Yakami no yama no
Kumoma yori
Watarau tsuki no

Although I longed for her—
As for the voyaging moon when it glides
  Into a rift of clouds
That swallow it up on Mount   30
  Yakami, where,

Oshikedo mo
Kakuroikureba
Amatsutau
Irihi sashinure

They say, men retire with their wives—
I took my lonely way, watching the sun
  Coursing through the sky
Till it sank behind the mountains.

Masurao to
Omoeru ware mo
Shikitae no
Koromo no sode wa
Tōrite nurenu.

Though I always thought   35
Myself a man with a warrior's heart,
  I found that my sleeves—
Wide as they were, like our bedclothes—
Were all soaked through with tears.

Envoys

Aogama no
Agaki o hayami
Kumoi ni zo
Imo ga atari o
Sugite kinikeru.

My gray-white horse
Has carried me at so swift a pace
  That I have left behind
The place where my beloved dwells
Beneath the cloudland of the distant sky.

Akiyama ni
Otsuru momijiba
Shimashiku wa
Na chirimagai so
Imo ga atari min.

O you yellow leaves
That whirl upon the autumn slopes—
  If only for a moment
Do not whirl down in such confusion,
That I may see where my beloved dwells.

In the poem's first section sea imagery predominates, in the second land imagery, in the third the imagery of the heavens. The vines of the second section recall the seaweed of the first, but without the sense of physical intimacy—indeed they convey a sense of parting which is completed by the image of the obscuring fall of autumn leaves. Terrestrial imagery dominates the second section, and celestial imagery the third. Each of these sections has a dominant mountain—Watari or Yakami—contrasted with the sea of love. Imagery of motion may be taken as a last example of imagistic strains and contrasts in the poem. In the first stanza there is a stasis or gentleness of movement appropriate to intimacy between husband and wife. Both characters move much more in the scene of parting in the second section, and such motions are transformed in the third to the symbolic moon for the wife and the sun for the husband.

At this point in the poem, having raised the concerns of his wife and himself to the celestial level, Hitomaro abruptly returns to personal feeling—to himself in tears. Had the poem ended with this, it would be emotionally and artistically flawed. The danger is soon averted, however, by the two envoys, which treat the experience of separation in terms midway between the celestial myth and the personal anguish, allowing Hitomaro to retain the generalizing symbolic force of the one and the intensity of personal emotion of the other. The first envoy covers most of the ground of the *chōka* very quickly by introducing the fast horse. Although it concludes with the celestial image of the cloudland, this image now implies a horizontal rather than a vertical distance; the emphasis is clearly on distance and separation. The second envoy treats the separation as an irreversible fact. In lines 23 and 24 of the *chōka,* the autumn leaves had already hidden his wife from sight; now he asks in vain for the leaves to stop falling. But what he really seeks, of course, is the abolishment of time and distance, two aspects of reality that are beautifully combined in a single image—*akiyama*, autumnal hill slopes. The last noun series in both envoys expresses what has been lost, "where my beloved dwells" (*imo ga atari*). It is toward this lost land that the poem leaves us looking; and insofar as we participate in the poet's experience, we see that the autumn whose leaves separate the lovers is both final and natural. Hitomaro saw such things plainly, even in his own affairs.

We read Hitomaro primarily for his *chōka*-envoy poems, but he also wrote separate *tanka* and *sedōka,* and it was these that were the more familiar to court poets in later periods. Most of the *tanka* have attractive imagery and flow melodiously, as is shown by the following poem from the "Hitomaro Collection" (*MYS,* VII: 1068).

Ame no umi ni	In the ocean of the sky
Kumo no nami tachi	Course the undulating waves of cloud,
Tsuki no fune	Rising by the moon-boat
Hoshi no hayashi ni	As it seems to disappear in rowing
Kogikakuru miyu.	Through the forest of the stars.

An agreeable poem, but one that cannot compare with the *tanka* of later periods, or with Hitomaro's own great *chōka*-envoy poems. This *tanka* is one of many poems in the *Man'yōshū* classified as "Poems on Things." The classification, which is Chinese, suggests that even at this early date poets—or was it only the compilers?— were already thinking in terms of set topics. We are almost certain that Hitomaro was inspired in his parallelism, and perhaps in his *chōka*-envoy form, by Chinese examples. But his greatness is far less a matter of his literary debt to China than of his Japanese insistence on historical and national continuity, his celebration of the land and people he loved, and his mature understanding of normal human life. He is one of those rare authors who, though we may know little of them personally, we feel we know completely as people. And he is also of that yet rarer kind whom we not only admire but love.

CHAPTER FOUR

Major Poets from 686 to 784

The sky into which Hitomaro rose like the sun had been neither wholly empty nor wholly dark. The long tradition of native oral song had been civilized by the example of Chinese poetry, and the general social and cultural advance—also inspired, in part, by the example of China—was such that it would have been reasonable to expect a great literature to emerge, one on a par with the sculpture of the day. Poetry does not come forth in full greatness, however, merely to meet our wishes or even our expectations. Japanese sculptors were fortunate in being able to understand without translation the accomplishments of visiting Koreans. The assimilation of the New Learning—a written language, religion, social philosophy, and poetic resources—from China was far more difficult, and all logic requires that numerous poets should have contributed to a slow and steady development. In fact, Hitomaro's greatest poems may have been nearly contemporary with the merely pleasant verse of Princess Nukata. Following the sudden efflorescence of Hitomaro's achievement, Japan was never without poets, and with his work Japan acquired a distinctive poetic tradition of the first order.

The contemporaries of Hitomaro have considerable appeal, diminished though it must be by his achievement. Takechi Furuhito and Takechi Kurohito (who may have been one person) seem almost to follow in his wake. One of two poems by Furuhito on "Grieving over the Ruins at Ōmi" (*MYS,* I: 32) reminds us of Hitomaro's far superior poem.*

* It is possible that "Furuhito" is a misprint for Kurohito, rising from a confusion due to the awkward manner of setting down poems in the *Man'yōshū*. At all events, next to nothing is known about Furuhito, and of Kurohito little is known beyond what is given in the text. He is thought to be roughly contemporaneous with Hitomaro, as his topical poems on the Ōmi capital would indicate.

Inishie no	I am not one
Hito ni ware are ya	Who lived through its glorious past,
Sasanami no	Yet here at Sasanami,
Furuki miyako o	As I look upon the ruined site,
Mireba kanashiki.	The lost capital claims my grief.

Kurohito has another, in my view better, poem on the subject (*MYS*, III: 305).

Kaku yue ni	I knew it would be so,
Miji to iu mono o	And even though I insisted to you
Sasanami no	That I would not look,
Furuki miyako o	You have made me look on Sasanami,
Misetsutsu mo to na.	Its capital lost in the waste of time.

Kurohito is an obscure figure; from his extant poems we can infer very little more than that he was a tireless traveler who wrote poems on the places he visited. One of them (*MYS*, III: 273), also set in the area that we know today as Lake Biwa, gives an idea of his gift for sketching scenes that convey movement and life.

Iso no saki	As we row along,
Kogitamiyukeba	Rounding the many rocky points
Ōmi no mi	On the Lake of Ōmi,
Yaso no minato ni	We come on anchorages by the score
Tazu sawa ni naku.	Where in their flocks the cranes cry out.

Such poems suggest what we had already inferred from Hitomaro's poems—that he was writing about subjects which also interested his contemporaries. Kurohito is a poet of some accomplishment, and although he lacks the scale and depth of Hitomaro, his writing makes the literary topography of the late seventh century more understandable by providing some fine foothills to the greater poet.

In the century following, Hitomaro's mark is easily recognizable, sometimes in subject matter, sometimes in technique. Sometimes we can see it in poems closely resembling his. In the sixth and ninth books of the *Man'yōshū,* there are a number of poems from "The Tanabe Sakimaro Collection," a title suggesting that Sakimaro was a poet of sufficient eminence to merit an early Japanese equivalent of our "collected works." Among the poems of Sakimaro (ca. 750) there is a *chōka* (without envoys) "On Seeing a Dead Man When Crossing the Pass of Ashigara" (*MYS,* IX: 1800), which calls to mind Hitomaro's Samine poem.

Okakitsu no	Your loving wife	
Asa o hikihoshi	No doubt spread out and bleached the threads	
Imonane ga	For your white hempen robe	
Tsukurikiseken	Upon the brushwood fence that stood about	
Shirotae no	Your modest eastern home.	5
Himo o mo tokazu	Perhaps she wove that robe for you to wear	
Hitoe yuu	In your labors for the court.	
Obi o mie yui	You must have toiled long, not stopping to untie	
Kurushiki ni	Your hempen belt for sleep,	
Tsukaematsurite	But winding it more tightly round your waist	10
Ima dani mo	Girded yourself not once but thrice.	
Kuni ni makarite	And then at last you earned a few brief days,	
Chichi haha mo	Time to set out for your home,	
Tsuma o mo min to	Thinking to see your parents and your wife.	
Omoitsutsu	At last you reached the east—	15
Yukiken kimi wa	Land of crowing cocks—you reached this pass,	
Tori ga naku	Awesome abode of gods.	
Azuma no kuni no	But in such rugged mountains	
Kashikoki ya	Your softly woven robe	
Kami no misaka ni	Could not have kept your wasted body warm;	20
Nikihada no	For you look cold,	
Koromo samura ni	With your hair as lustrous black	
Nubatama no	As jewels of jet	
Kami wa midarete	Lying loose and tangled round about you.	
Kuni toedo	Though I speak to you	25
Kuni o mo norazu	To ask about your native land,	
Ie toedo	You do not reply;	
Ie o mo iwazu	And though I ask you of your home,	
Masurao no	You do not speak,	
Yuki no manimani	But lie outstretched, courageous man,	30
Koko ni koyaseru.	Asleep forever on your journey home.	

Two things about Sakimaro's *chōka* are striking—its almost photographic imagery and its resemblance to the last third of Hitomaro's Samine poem. The particularity reveals the fullness with which Sakimaro has imagined and re-created the scene. We are struck by the pathos, but we are not really involved in it, for by comparison with the other poem, this one merely provides effective realism. We lack that shared experience of danger which brings the dead man and the narrator together before us as men like ourselves. We lack the overture extolling the divine land and putting events into a wider setting. And although Sakimaro has a fluid, skillful style, he lacks the mature vision of Hitomaro. There is so little certainty about Sakimaro's dates—and Hitomaro's, too, for that matter—that we cannot know certainly whether Hitomaro made great what Sakimaro had made good, or whether Sakimaro imitated Hitomaro less successfully. We can see differences in quality, however, and can understand common impulses behind the subjects shared by Kurohito, Sakimaro, and Hitomaro. The age had acquired a literary momentum.

After Hitomaro, there are, however, three poets of the first rank, each entitled to the claim that he created in his poetry a world or an ethos recognizably his own and different from what had gone before. The three are Yamanoe Okura (?660–?733), Yamabe Akahito (?d. 736), and Ōtomo Yakamochi (718–85). Of the three, Okura's personality is the most complex. He is a strict moralist, and yet sentimental about children. He is free with criticism of others, and yet deeply sympathetic toward the unfortunate. His style is crabbed and knotty, and yet in the first envoy to his "Elegy on the Death of Furuhi" (*MYS*, V: 905), he wrote what a French critic thought the most sublime poem in the language. Okura's son has died and must go to the underworld.

Wakakereba	Since he is so young,
Michiyuki shiraji	He will not know the road to take:
Mai wa sen	I will pay your fee—
Shitabe no tsukai	O courier from the realms below,
Oite tōrase.	Bear him there upon your back!

The fragmented syntax of the original is somehow made to sing a father's grief for his dead child and a continuing concern that

58

cannot accept the fact of death. Such grief is a universal response, but the death of one's own children is less often expressed in the public light of poetry than in private tears. Okura's success is therefore an artistic success in rendering all too common experience in uncommon poetry.

His "Dialogue on Poverty" (*MYS*, V: 892–93) is very different. It reveals that he felt for others a sympathy akin to the love he had for his son, and it expresses a concern with society that recasts Hitomaro's public poetry into an ethos completely Okura's own.

THE POOR MAN

Kaze majie	On those dreary nights	
Ame furu yo no	When rain falls freezing in the wind,	
Ame majie	On such bitter nights	
Yuki furu yo wa	When snow falls mixed with freezing drizzle,	
Sube mo naku	I have no better comfort	5
Samuku shi areba	In the onslaught of the numbing cold	
Katashio o	Than to sit and nibble	
Toritsuzushiroi	On this poor lump of blackened salt	
Kasuyuzake	And sip from time to time	
Uchisusuroite	Upon this wretched brew of *sake* lees.	10
Shiwabukai	Then as my body warms	
Hana bishibishi ni	I clear my throat and sniffle,	
Shika to aranu	As I glow with drink	
Hige kakinadete	I stroke the straggly hairs of my beard,	
Are o okite	Declaring to myself:	15
Hito wa araji to	"There is no one worth thinking about	
Hokoroedo	—Apart, of course, from me."	
Samuku shi areba	But in the face of the numbing cold	
Asabusuma	I still draw up about me	
Hikikagafuri	My thin bedding of paltry hemp,	20
Nuno kataginu	And pile on in layers	
Ari no kotogoto	Every thin fiber vest I own—	
Kisoedo mo	And still I shudder,	
Samuki yo sura o	So bitter is the freezing night.	
Ware yori mo	So what of you,	25
Mazushiki hito no	Whose wretchedness is worse than mine?	
Chichi haha wa	Your father and your mother	

59

Uekogoyuran	Must be famished in the bitter cold,
Me kodomo wa	Your wife and children
Niyobinaku ran	Can only sob and whine in pain. 30
Kono toki wa	In times as hard as these
Ika ni shitsutsu ka	By what devices do such as you
Na ga yo wa wataru.	Make shift to endure your lives?

THE DESTITUTE MAN

Ame tsuchi wa	Though the saying goes
Hiroshi to iedo	That the heavens and earth are vast, 35
Aga tame wa	My experience is
Saku ya narinuru	That they have shrunk upon me.
Hi tsuki wa	And though the saying is
Akashi to iedo	That the sun and moon are radiant,
Aga tame wa	My experience is 40
Teri ya tamawanu	That they have failed to shine on me.
Hito mina ka	Do all men suffer so,
Are nomi ya shikaru	Or is this the case with me alone?
Wakuraba ni	With blessed fortune
Hito to wa aru o	I was born in this world as a man, 45
Hitonami ni	And in the fields
Are mo tsukuru o	I have worked as hard as any,
Wata mo naki	And yet my clothes
Nuno kataginu no	Consist of this one unpadded vest
Miru no goto	Of coarse hempen fiber 50
Wawakesagareru	Hanging across and down my shoulders,
Kakafu nomi	Dangling all in tatters
Kata ni uchikake	No better than ragged strips of kelp.
Fuseio no	My house is a hovel,
Mageio no uchi ni	Low-roofed and half fallen in, 55
Hitatsuchi ni	With cold bare earth
Wara tokishikite	Beneath the scattered straw.
Chichi haha wa	In the seat above
Makura no kata ni	My father and mother crouch,
Me kodomo wa	While down below 60
Ato no kata ni	My wife and children lie
Kakumiite	And press about me,
Uesamayoi	Groaning in their wretchedness.
Kamado ni wa	Upon the hearth
Hoke fukitatezu	No fire sends up its smoke, 65
Koshiki ni wa	And in the pot

60

Kumo no su kakite	Only a spider drapes its web—
Ii kashiku	We have forgotten
Koto mo wasurete	Even the manner of cooking food,
Nuedori no	And like the night finch 70
Nodo yoioru ni	We raise weak-throated cries.
Ito nokite	Yet this is not all.
Mijikaki mono o	For to cap our misery, to cut—
Hashi kiru to	As the saying goes—
Ieru ga gotoku	What was already short still shorter, 75
Shimoto toru	The growling voice
Satoosa ga koe wa	Of the tax collector with his stick
Neyado made	Even disrupts our sleep,
Kitachiyobainu	As he stands threatening at the door.
Kaku bakari	Must life be only this, 80
Sube naki mono ka	So hopelessly beyond our powers?
Yo no naka no michi.	Is this the way of the world?

Envoy

THE POET

Yo no naka o	One of us may feel
Ushi to yasashi to	That life holds only pain, and another
Omoedo mo	That our lot is shameful, 85
Tobitachikanetsu	Yet since we are not birds, but men,
Tori ni shi araneba.	We cannot find escape in flight.

The style is rough, with an obtrusive parallelism and a jerky, elbowy movement not unlike the "strong lines" of Donne and satirists contemporary with him. The intense parallelism and the crabbed style help convey a sense of commitment and the misery of the speakers (again like Donne), and both stylistic features assist the formation of single lines into larger passages (see, for example, lines 54–63 in Japanese). Such stylistic characteristics are found as well in other poems by Okura. What is unquestionably unusual is the criticism of the fabric of society. In its implications of social protest, the poem is simply unparalleled in Japanese poetry until modern times. Okura's experience in China and with Chinese poetry had acquainted him with the political admonitions to the throne that the literati of China often wrote. In Confucian theory, such injustice in the state betokens poor rule; the ruler must change his ways. Three elements dilute the strength of Okura's protest, however. To begin with, not even Okura could afford to suggest that the virtues of the unbroken imperial line had disappeared. Consequently he chooses a Japanese indirection, criticizing the village headman come for taxes on the one hand and lamenting the general human condition on the other. If such an emphasis on village life avoids criticism of the imperial arcanum, it also precludes the Confucian scheme of rational political philosophy and avoids the actualities of Japanese politics. But what may be thought deficient in social protest is more than compensated for by the particularity which creates so moving a drama of men facing poverty. The rather anticlimactic envoy offers no consolation—we are returned to the fact of our miserable humanity. The third element is precisely the human drama of the poem. So moving a representation of the suffering brought by poverty renders political didacticism unnecessary. There are some motifs common to the outbursts of the Poor Man and the Destitute Man, notably an indoor-outdoor contrast, a concern with food and clothes, and a persistent self-examination. The Poor Man, perhaps like Okura himself, is proud and angry, yet also ironic at his own expense. As he sits nibbling salt, sipping unappealing drink, and pulling on his unimpressive beard, he shows a concern with those who are yet worse off than he. The Destitute Man is given even more effective poetry. There is the sweep from heaven and earth and sun and moon (34–41), across the fields tilled (42–47), indoors to the man himself and his family (48–63), and at last to the food pot with its symbolic spider web (64–71). The headman coming for taxes provides a superfluous and gratuitous torment at this stage. The Destitute Man and his family cannot even suffer in peace. The worry, the ache of hunger, and the resentment brought by poverty are all well brought out by the poem. Is there, then, nothing to be done (*Sube naki mono ka?*) about man's lot? The answer to the question is very Japanese. One can cry out over a misery from which one cannot escape. When in one sense nothing can be done, one can still assert one's humanity by saying that the pain hurts.

Okura's pessimism is in some respects yet more marked in his

"Lament on the Instability of Human Life" (*MYS*, V: 804–5), which insists even more strongly on the suffering human condition, and, therefore, on the naturalness of man's crying hurt at his lot.

Yo no naka no	Life is such in this world	
Sube naki mono wa	That our struggles are all in vain:	
Toshi tsuki wa	Years rise on months	
Nagaruru gotoshi	And time flows ever onward,	
Toritsutsuki	Flooding us away;	5
Oikuru mono wa	A hundred trivial concerns	
Momokusa ni	Oppress us in succession	
Semeyorikitaru	And stifle us under their weight.	
Otomera ga	So women bent with age	
Otomesabisu to	Once rejoiced in being young—	10
Karatama o	Carefree girls binding,	
Tamoto ni makashi	As girls are ever known to do,	
Shirotae no	Binding foreign jewels	
Sode furikawashi	About their gaily draped arms—	
Kurenai no	Waving white linen sleeves,	15
Akamo susobiki	Trailing the hems of scarlet skirts	
Yochikora to	As hand in hand they went,	
Te tazusawarite	Spending their time in happy play,	
Asobiken	And all were girls together.	
Toki no sakari o	But time has the power of seasons,	20
Todomikane	And irresistibly	
Sugushiyaritsure	Summer has given way to winter;	
Mina no wata	And at an unremembered hour	
Kaguroki kami ni	Those glistening tresses, black	
Itsu no ma ka	As the mud-snail's innards,	25
Shimo no furiken	Were whitened by a silent frost;	
Kurenai no	As from a time obscure	
Omote no ue ni	Those cheeks that glowed so bright,	
Izuku yu ka	Those scarlet cheeks,	
Shiwa ga kitarishi	Were wrinkled-scratched by time.	30
Masurao no	So the bold young men	
Otokosabisu to	Rejoiced to prove their manliness:	
Tsurugi tachi	Like warriors girded their hips	

Koshi ni torihaki	With their straight or curving swords,
Satsuyumi o	Clutched tightly in their hands 35
Tanigirimochite	Their deadly, beast-destroying bows,
Akagoma ni	Threw upon their roans
Shitsukura uchioki	Saddles of woven workmanship,
Hainorite	Climbed upon their mounts,
Asobiarukishi	And eagerly galloped away to the hunt. 40

Yo no naka ya	But is the way of the world
Tsune ni arikeru	Such that these moments can long endure?
Otomera ga	For a night of love
Sanasu itado o	The eager girls quietly push open
Oshihiraki	Their wooden doors, 45
Itadoriyorite	And their lovers grope, then clasp
Matamade no	The hands they sought,
Tamade sashikae	And sleep, beloved arms entwined.

Saneshi yo no	But such nights are few,
Ikuda mo araneba	And soon the lover goes with age's 50
	hand-staff
Tatsukazue	Carried by his side,
Koshi ni taganete	And then goes stumbling onward,
Ka yukeba	Scorned by the passerby;
Hito ni itowae	He must go stumbling endlessly,
Kaku yukeba	Despised by passing crowds. 55
Hito ni nikumae	For such is the common course of life,
Oyoshio wa	That age should bring
Kaku nomi narashi	Just this much and nothing more—
Tamakiwaru	That we cling to life
Inochi oshikedo	As long as our souls endure it, 60
Sen sube mo nashi.	And our efforts are all in vain.

Envoy

Tokiwa nasu	How I yearn to be
Kaku shi mo ga mo to	Unalterably what once I was,
Omoedo mo	Immovable as a rock,
Yo no koto nareba	But because I belong to this world,
Todomikanetsu mo.	There is no stop to time.

The first and last sections of the *chōka*, and the envoy as well, generalize in a way peculiar to Okura among court poets. Rarity does not guarantee its complete success, unfortunately, and most readers will respond more fully to the vivid scenes of girls growing up, of young men showing their masculinity, of eager lovers, and of despised age. Okura himself obviously loved human activity. How well he shows masculine bemusement over that air girls have of walking off in mysterious hand-holding societies. Similarly, he moves us with the picture of young men emulating the bravery of their elders in the hunt, and of the joy of lovers' nights. And yet—

> . . . is the way of the world
> Such that these moments can long endure?

The enemy is time: "And our efforts are all in vain."

The organization of the poem adds powerfully to the sense of irresistible, irreversible time, a theme that is implied in the generalizations at the beginning (1–8) and end (49–61) of the *chōka* and stated explicitly in the envoy. In between, Okura earns the poet's right to generalize by his carefully ordered particularities. The first scene (9–30) portrays girls not yet at the age to love men or to enter into the world of women. The second scene (31–40) describes young men progressing to full adolescence; they may not be old enough to be lovers or to assume full responsibility, but they can enter into a sport, the hunt, resembling the war of their fathers. In the next section (41–48), Okura returns to the girls, who are now of an age to love, and to them he joins the young men of a similar age.

> And their lovers grope, then clasp
> The hands they sought,
> And sleep, beloved arms entwined.

They have fully realized the best that life can give, and they sleep with the happiness of fulfillment and of sharing oneself with another human being. But while they sleep, time passes, and age seems suddenly to come, like an unexpected early frost.

The contrast between the joy before and the pain afterward is conveyed by contrasting images of parts of the human body. While there is still happiness, the image is that of hands or arms (the Japanese word is the same for both):

Binding foreign jewels
About their gaily draped arms

. . .

As hand in hand they went,
Spending their time in happy play

. . .

Clutched tightly in their hands
Their deadly, beast-destroying bows

. . .

For a night of love
The eager girls quietly push open
Their wooden doors,
And their lovers grope, then clasp
The hands they sought,
And sleep, beloved arms entwined.

The last passage is obviously the climax of the poem, bringing together the girls and boys treated separately in the earlier passages. But to what end does the climax of the poem focus on hands (or arms)? Surely it is because Okura sought a way to emphasize human action, pleasure, and even communication without introducing speech as he did in "Dialogue on Poverty." He wishes to emphasize in his "Lament" man's utter lack of awareness, of thought, even of expression concerning his fate. He generalizes the unself-consciousness that adults see in childhood and youth. It is appropriate that he contrasts the active hand-arm images for youth with more passive images for old age—the black hair turned white, the scarlet cheeks scratched with wrinkles, the aged accompanied by the lifeless staff.

There are two seeming exceptions to this pattern of contrasted images. The first is the image of young men with swords at their hips—an image corresponding to that of the old person limping with a staff at the side. But as the Japanese original of the passage makes clear, the point is that the act of the young men is precisely designed to get them to adulthood (*Otokosabisu to / Tsurugi tachi / Koshi ni torihaki*); the exception therefore fits thematically. The other exception comes after the climax:

But such nights are few,
And soon the lover goes with age's hand-staff
Carried at his side.

66

The lines recall the passage on the young men, of course, but in stressing that it is a hand-staff (*tatsukazue*), the poet also recalls the immediately preceding passage on the lovers. The image provides both a transition (prepared for by the shift in attention from girls to boys in the preceding lines) and an ironic theme: the hands' joys have come to this, "And our efforts are all in vain."

Okura's poetry invites such scrutiny by virtue of both its highly individual style and its technique, and it offers at its best a convincing if deeply pessimistic view of life. The pessimism admits all the evidence of happiness; it even welcomes sentiment; and it is tinged by a strong moral view. But whereas Hitomaro looked on tragedy and praised human dignity in a complex world, Okura looked on the beauty and joy he loved and saw it ruined by human injustice and forces even farther beyond man's control. We may well feel with Japanese readers that Okura's world leaves us highly chastened in our expectations of life but more deeply appreciative of what we have to lose.

The ethos of Akahito's poetry is far happier. He loves to praise and to enjoy scenes from which he stands somewhat apart as an observer, a spectator. He protects himself against the challenges reckoned with by Hitomaro and the shocks felt by Okura by retaining an insulating distance from experience. One of his *tanka* uses the images for young men and women that Okura had used for girls and boys. Yet what a difference there is in his tone (*MYS*, VI: 1001).

Masurao wa	The noble warriors
Mikari ni tatashi	Set forth upon the royal hunt,
Otomera wa	While their ladies
Akamo susobiku	Trail their scarlet skirts
Kiyoki hamabi o.	Along the clean-swept beach.

Akahito beautifully contrasts the warriors' energetic movement inland or into the background of the poem, with the light stepping back and forth of the ladies in the foreground of the beach. The beach is *kiyoki*; more than clean-swept, it is pure, unsullied, fresh. And so is the world Akahito loves.

The greatest threats admitted to his world are surprise and mystery, but these are easily absorbed to heighten the purity and beauty, as we see in his envoy to "On a Distant View of Mount

67

Fuji" (*MYS*, III: 318), the most famous of all poems on the subject. He comes upon the mountain suddenly.

Tago no ura yu	Along the Tago coast
Uchiidete mireba	We come out to the open and see it—
Mashiro ni zo	How white it is!
Fuji no takane ni	The lofty cone of Fuji sparkling
Yuki wa furikeru.	Beneath its newly fallen snow.

Both the world of human affairs and the natural world in which man finds himself bring joy to Akahito. No other court poet seems to have found the world more to his liking. What the court could create and what it could adapt from the natural world are equally praised in his poems on the Yoshino Palace, one of which (*MYS*, VI: 923–25) concludes with two very appealing *tanka* envoys.

Yasumishishi	To our great Sovereign	
Wago ōkimi no	Who rules over all the land in peace	
Taka shirasu	Belongs this lofty palace,	
Yoshino no miya wa	Majestic Yoshino, divinely built.	
Tatanazuku	Range high on range,	5
Aokakigomori	Green mountain walls enshrine it,	
Kawanami no	While pure and clear	
Kiyoki kōchi zo	Flow the waters of the stream.	
Harube wa	In the springtime	
Hana sakiōri	Flowers blossom on the mountain walls,	10
Aki sareba	And with the autumn	
Kiri tachiwataru	Banners of mist hover in the sky.	
Sono yama no	Again and yet again,	
Iya masumasu ni	Like the mountains range on range	
Kono kawa no	And never ceasing,	15
Tayuru koto naku	Like the stream that ever flows,	
Momoshiki no	The courtiers will come	
Ōmiyabito wa	In reverent corps to these imperial halls	
Tsune ni kayowan.	Erected on foundations multi-walled.	

Envoys

Mi-Yoshino no	From among the branches
Kisayama no ma no	Of the trees upon Mount Kisa's slopes,
Konure ni wa	The flocks of birds
Kokoda mo sawaku	Fill the lovely vale of Yoshino
Tori no koe ka mo.	With their free and joyous songs.

Nubatama no	The jet-black night
Yo no fukeyukeba	Deepens to a hush among the birches
Hisaki ouru	In the stream's pure bed,
Kiyoki kawara ni	Where the plovers raise their call
Chidori shiba naku.	Above the murmur of the stream.

Again, in the *chōka* and in the second envoy, there is the word "pure" (*kiyoki*). The world is fresh, beautiful, immaculate. The influence of Shintoism pervades the poem and becomes explicit in the *chōka*, which describes the palace in terms of the natural setting of a Shinto shrine. The parallelism of the *chōka* suggests an element of poetic constraint, however, that is absent from the envoys. We can understand why, in the Preface to the *Kokinshū*, Tsurayuki—who knew only their *tanka* poetry—found it impossible to rate Akahito beneath Hitomaro or Hitomaro above Akahito.

Ours is an easier decision. We observe the combination of thinness and schematic structure in the *chōka*: such bones are beautiful, but to use a comparison of the kind Tsurayuki liked, they need more flesh, like a beautiful but famished child. The *tanka* are beyond any specific criticism. Truly they are beautiful and make the world seem wonderful. Would we really be wiser—would it really satisfy us more fully—to engage more closely with the world only to find that such precious beauty was put in jeopardy? In reading Akahito's poems, we shrink from the test, but in the end we feel some uneasiness that he has chosen to stand off from the world, to hold experience at arm's length. Are we right to feel this way? Every other major court poet would say we were. It is true that most Japanese see in the poetry of the *Man'yōshū* qualities of brightness, purity, sincerity, integrity, and easy accommodation with the world. They see what Akahito saw. But it is a measure of the greater range and profundity of Hitomaro, Okura, and Yakamochi that their poetry encompasses the sullied as well as the pure, the unbearable as well as the happy. And yet most Japanese rank Akahito without reservation among the truly great Japanese poets.

One reason for the admiration of Akahito is the beauty of his style. Another and much more important reason is the ease with which he encompasses many subjects. Looking closely at the poem

on the Yoshino Palace, we discover that he has, after all, been talking about man and nature, about the imperial line and the functioning court, about time, architecture, and religion. These subjects
enter so naturally, so unobtrusively, that it seems almost pedantic
to mention them. They come in by parallelisms and contrasts
(mountains, streams; spring, autumn), and we are more aware
of the parallelism than of a literary subject. Or it may be simply
a pillow-word—"Erected on foundations multi-walled" (*Momo-
shiki no*)—that by its conventional nature almost as much as by
its residual image suggests art, the artist, and man's endeavors.
In other words, there is no reason to question the breadth of experience behind Akahito's awareness, or even the breadth touched
on in this poem. Because Akahito's sophistication is obvious, it is
all the more remarkable that he should concern himself with beautiful simplicities. For example, his other poems on the Yoshino
court (*MYS*, VI: 926–27) take their delight in the court's hunting
parties. Instead of the personalities of Hitomaro's court poems, we
have an animated pageantry—activity rather than active people.
Being Akahito, he dwells on the scene as well as its life, as isolated
lines show: "On the morning hunt," "On the evening hunt," "On
the moors," "On the tangled moors of spring." He looks at much,
reports on part of it, and seems to think much, say little, and do
less. There is almost nothing in Akahito's work like the full participation of Hitomaro in the experience of the dead man on Samine, little of the passionate engagement of Okura, and little even
of the lesser poetic involvement of Kurohito declaring, "I was
there."

Akahito obviously represents an extreme example of the urge to
celebration in Japanese poetry, and his silences suggest what pure
celebration may cost. He is finally a baffling poet, not for any obscurity but for the very simplicity he insists on, the beauty he *will*
write of. We know almost nothing about him, certainly not
enough to explain why he is the kind of poet he is. He can be
seen as the inverse of Okura. To achieve his aim of celebration,
Akahito was obliged to stand back at some distance from people,
from life. He had either to rise above or to conceal the personalities of those he wrote about. He was led to speak with enthusiasm
of some things but with the utmost reserve of others. Okura, in

contrast, has at times too little reserve and therefore may lapse into didacticism or sentimentality. But he is always committed. Together, these poets show by their excesses or deficiencies that Hitomaro's balance between his inner and outer worlds, between man and nature, between self and society, was indeed something of a miracle. To be sure, in Japanese as in other poetic traditions, the greatest poetry has two subjects, which are seen both separately and in relation to each other: human existence and the world in which man finds himself. By this standard, the work of Okura and Akahito is limited, Okura's with its emphasis on man's moral and emotional responses, Akahito's with its emphasis on aesthetic appreciation. And yet the finest poems of both achieve greatness by excelling in their less than total aims—Okura's by the justice of their response, Akahito's by the fineness of their discrimination.

Ōtomo Yakamochi—the last of the great *Man'yōshū* poets and one of the collection's compilers—is a much less baffling poet than Akahito; he is as interested in exploring (and therefore revealing) his personality as Akahito is in concealing his. Well-bred, widely experienced in life and literature, conscious of history and of individual human lives, Yakamochi emerges as a very attractive if slightly bookish man. And emerge he does—in poetry and to some extent historically. For if not much is known of him and his family, what little we do know amounts almost to more than we know of the other major *Man'yōshū* poets put together. The Ōtomo clan had for centuries been connected with the court. They had served as bodyguards for the emperor; they were noble retainers, the military élite. Several of Yakamochi's ancestors were famous in their day: one was sent as envoy to the Korean state of Silla in 530; another was the seventh-century courtier, Suguri, who perfected the art of invisibility; still another was the court intriguer, Kanamura. By the eighth century, however, the power was fading, and the glory had to be recalled. Akahito may have chosen to stand aloof from power, but the Ōtomo clan was being cut off from it. Such circumstances have again and again brought forth the finest of Japanese poets, and although there are more than a dozen other poets in the *Man'yōshū* who belong to the Ōtomo clan, it was Yakamochi more than the rest, or more than any other poet at all, who brought glory to the end of the early literary period.

He did so by introducing reflection, something like Hitomaro's concern with public and personal experience, with something like Akahito's reserve. But the reserve of Yakamochi is more a mental process of subjectivity than a careful stance. Where other poets, even Akahito, had looked outward, Yakamochi looked inward, bringing a subjectivity to court poetry that was to dominate it from that time on. If we are slow to see this change in his poetry, it is because at first we are altogether taken by his variety. There are elegies, a poem on the discovery of gold in Michinoku (MYS, XVIII: 4094–97), poems of gallantry to the Elder Daughter of Lady Ōtomo of Sakanoe, poems written as if by the humble or by Yakamochi's close friends, and poems describing his garden. The element common to all these is reflective musing. In a passage of the poem on the discovery of gold, Yakamochi thinks back on the glories of his clan.

Tōtsu kamuoya no	Those remote forebears who so gloriously
Sono na o ba	Bore their proud name—
Ōkumenushi to	"Great lords of Kume," they were called—
Oimochite	And swore their fealty,
Tsukaeshi tsukasa	Vowing to serve their gracious sovereign:
Umi yukaba	"When we venture on the sea,
Mitsuku kabane	Then may our corpses soak in the brine,
Yama yukaba	When we cross high mountains,
Kusamusu kabane	Then from our bodies let wild grasses grow,
Ōkimi no	For we will not look back
He ni koso shiname.	If only we may die beside our lord!"

It is an attractive re-creation of the glories of the past, but those who had power at court no longer looked to the Ōtomo clan for valor. The poet's reflective bent is even more marked in his personal poems, and much of this introspection can be represented by the footnote to his "Poem of Joy Composed When He Dreamed of His Stray Hawk" (MYS, XVII: 4011–15).

In the village of Furue, Imizu District, a hawk was caught. It was perfect in form and matchless in ferocity. Yamada Kimimaro, the hawker, lacked perfect care in training it, and used it out of season. It soared up and flew away and could by no means be brought back. With nets spread out it was watched for, many prayers were made, with offerings, and I trusted to chance. A girl appeared in a dream and said: "Good Sir, do not be distressed, nor let your heart so pine! The stray hawk will be caught before long." I awoke and joy revived in me. Therefore in response to the dream I composed a poem to put away my sorrows.*

No earlier poet had written such introspective poetry, poetry about so subjectively personal an event. Yet the treatment is different from that by later poets. The opening lines of the *chōka* give the private experience of losing a favorite hawk the public setting of Yakamochi's duties in Koshi province. The poet combines what is in theory impossible—the public with the private mode—and this combination is the distinguishing feature of his longer poems. The public element relates him to his age; the private is new as a really significant quality and points ahead to later poetry. The peculiar blend can be seen in the "Lament" he composed for his son-in-law, Fujiwara Toyonari, whose mother had just died (*MYS*, XIX: 4214–16).

Ame tsuchi no	Since that ancient time	
Hajime no toki yu	When the heavens and earth began,	
Utsusomi no	It has been decreed	
Yasotomo no o wa	That of the eighty noble clans	
Ōkimi ni	Each living man	5
Matsurou mono to	Shall follow obediently the commands	
Sadamareru	Of our great Sovereign.	
Tsukasa ni shi areba	So I, an official of the court,	
Ōkimi no	Heard with veneration	
Mikoto kashikomi	The sacred words of our great	10
	Sovereign;	
Hinazakaru	And now I live,	
Kuni o osamu to	Governing this distant province	
Ashihiki no	Here in the wilds,	

* Translation from *Manyōshū: One Thousand Poems* (Tokyo, 1940; New York and London, 1965), p. 149.

Yama kawa henari	Cut off from home by hills and streams.
Kaze kumo ni	Since my coming here 15
Koto wa kayoedo	You and I have had but winds and clouds
Tada ni awazu	To bear our messages;
Hi no kasanareba	And as days have piled on days and still
Omoikoi	We have not met again,
Ikizukioru ni	I have longed to see you more and more, 20
Tamahoko no	And sighed with yearning.
Michi kuru hito no	Straight as a jeweled spear
Tsutegoto ni	Was the road he came on,
Ware ni kataraku	The traveler who has brought these tidings:
Hashiki yoshi	He reports that you, 25
Kimi wa kono goro	My amiable and noble friend,
Urasabite	Are struck in grief
Nagekaiimasu	And lately spend your days in mourning.
Yo no naka no	Truly the span of life
Ukeku tsurakeku	Is filled with sorrow and suffering: 30
Saku hana mo	The very flowers open
Toki ni utsurou	Only to wither and fall with time,
Utsusemi mo	And we living men
Tsune naku arikeri	Are creatures of a like impermanence.
Tarachine no	Surely it must be 35
Mioya no mikoto	That even your most noble mother,
Nani shi ka mo	At whose breasts you fed,
Toki shi wa aran o	Must like others have a fatal hour.
Masokagami	And now this news:
Miredo mo akazu	That in the full bloom of her 40
	womanhood,
	When one might still gaze
Tama no o no	Upon her beauty with such rare delight
Oshiki sakari ni	As on a polished mirror,
Tatsu kiri no	Cherishing her like a string of jewels,
Useyuku gotoku	Even she has faded away, 45
Oku tsuyu no	Vanished like the rising mists,
Kenuru ga goto	Like dew upon the grass;
Tamamo nasu	That she lay listless as the gem-like seaweed
Nabikikoifushi	Bending to the tide;
Yuku mizu no	That like a running stream she ebbed 50
Todomikanetsu to	away

74

Magakoto ya	And could not be held back.
Hito no iitsuru	Can this be some fantastic tale I hear?
Oyozure o	Is not the message false,
Hito no tsugetsuru	Merely a rumor of a passing traveler?
Azusayumi	Though from afar— 55
Tsuma hiku yo to no	Like the warning of bowstrings twanged
Tōto ni mo	By palace guards at night—
Kikeba kanashimi	I hear this news, my grief is fresh,
Niwatazumi	And I cannot keep
Nagaruru namida	The tears from flowing down my cheeks 60
Todomikanetsu mo.	Like rivulets from a sudden shower.

Envoys

Tōto ni mo	This news I hear,
Kimi ga nageku to	That you, my friend, are plunged in grief,
Kikitsureba	Comes from afar,
Ne nomi shi nakayu	But still I must raise my voice in weeping:
Aimou ware wa.	Your distant sorrow weighs upon my heart.

Yo no naka no	You know as I
Tsune naki koto wa	The nature of this illusory world,
Shiru ran o	How nothing stays—
Kokoro tsukusu na	Endeavor to be brave and stalwart,
Masurao ni shite.	Do not wear out that heart in grief.

In the first section of the poem (1–21) Yakamochi begins with a version of Hitomaro's overtures, goes on to tell of his own imperial service, and before we know it is speaking of his private emotions. The next section (22–54) similarly begins with a broader view of the external world—the long road traveled by the messenger—before turning to a private subject, Toyonari's mother, who is compared to the mirrors (in all probability imported from China) that were of great price at this time and to those gems which to Japanese have particularly feminine associations. The third section of the *chōka* (55–61) goes to the external world again—the twanging of bowstrings by the palace guards back in the capital—for an experience that leads to tears of private grief. The image of the guards effectively implies a sense of manifold loss—the overt one of Toyonari's mother, and the implicit ones of Yakamochi's isolation from the capital and his military clan's past glories. The public and private emphases merge, harmonize, and accommodate each other. So capacious is Yakamochi's poetic world that he can include in it the generalizations of Okura about human misery, the celebrations of Hitomaro of the human and divine, and yet always seem to be most interested in his own apprehension of these things. As this description may suggest, Yakamochi is by far the most modern of the poets of the *Man'yōshū*.

Yakamochi's poetry has one serious limitation: it lacks intensity. One seldom finds in his poems a concentration of utterance, a sudden flowering of emotion, or a full crystallizing of experience. His poems are memorable more for the moods they express than for a sharply described experience. Having said this, we must also grant Yakamochi his virtues, of which one of the most enduring is the mellowness of his style. Stylistic assessments imply comparison with other poets and demand knowledge of the poet's own language. Even the best translation could not do justice to the resonance of Yakamochi's style, which is mellifluous without being lax, and strong without being harsh. It is a music harmonizing the numerous possible discords between the public and private worlds he somehow reconciles. It is, finally, a style that like its creator grows steadily in appeal as one's own tastes become more informed and one's experience richer.

There is also in Yakamochi's poetry a stillness bred of reflection that reminds one of Wordsworth among English poets, vastly different though the two are in most other respects. Matthew Arnold spoke of Wordsworth's "healing power," a phrase that applies with equal justice to Yakamochi, whose poems give a rare and quiet refreshment. There are three spring poems (*MYS*, XIX: 4290–92) of private musing that give special pleasure because their creator has mastered the essential literary art of pleasing others while pleasing himself.

Haru no no ni	Across spring fields
Kasumi tanabiki	The haze drifts along in banners
Uraganashi	Pleasing to the heart,
Kono yūkage ni	And in the dusk a warbler
Uguisu naku mo.	Sings out amid the crimson light.

76

Wa ga yado no	From my garden
Isasa murateke	Where bamboo stands in little clusters,
Fuku kaze no	Faintly comes the sound
Oto no kasokeki	Of the leaves that rustle darkly
Kono yūbe ka mo.	In the breeze of this spring dusk.

Uraura ni	The lark flies up
Tereru harubi ni	Into a sky glowing with the light
Hibari agari	Of a fair spring day,
Kokoro kanashi mo	And I alone stand here to feel it
Hitori shi omoeba.	Bring such gladness to the heart.

So mellow is the style, so harmonious are the elements of the poems, that we are apt to miss such local felicities as "leaves that rustle darkly" (*Oto no kasokeki*).

Poems of this sort are at once private and formal, being written with great art for general reading. It is when Yakamochi is most private, as we have seen, that he most clearly forecasts the future of court poetry. The verses of witty wooing exchanged with the Elder Daughter of Lady Ōtomo of Sakanoe bear the seeds of the later poetry of gallantry and courtly love. And the questioning of reality that was later to become an obsession of court poets is prefigured in a poem he wrote about his garden (*MYS,* XIX: 4140).

Waga sono no	Fallen in my garden,
Sumomo no hana ka	Are they blossoms of the damson trees
Niwa ni furu	Standing in the courtyard,
Hadare no imada	Or patches of lately fallen snow
Nokoritaru ka mo.	Lingering whitely on the ground?

Yakamochi is at his best, however, when he is neither old- nor new-fashioned but merely himself in his own time expressing what is most significant to him. Again and again we discover an inward-looking reflective vision in his poetry, a public world flowing through his own stream of consciousness, and a personal quiet that yet welcomes other human beings. It is not one of his major poems, but another *tanka,* "On Seeing the Blossoms of the Peach and Damson Trees" (*MYS,* XIX: 4139), shows what such vision can create.

77

Haru no sono	In the spring garden,
Kurenai niou	The peach trees are filled with flowers
Momo no hana	Whose pink color
Shitaderu michi ni	Brightens the little path below
Idetatsu otome.	Where a woman now steps forth.

Earlier poets had not been able to discover in their own gardens a subject of sufficient reality or importance for poetry. Later poets would leave out the figure of the woman on the path, replacing her with their own subjective consciousness or with symbols.

If we substitute for that woman Yakamochi himself, and imagine the spring to be that of Japanese poetry, then the poem is a fair description of his place in it. By the time of Yakamochi, Japanese poetry had proved itself. It was capable of producing great poets and compilers. And it was capable of development. The spring sunshine in which Yakamochi stepped forth brightened the first splendid age of court poetry, which was no less precious a time for the promise it held of successive seasons of growth and maturity.

CHAPTER FIVE

Major Poets from 784 to 1100

The *Man'yōshū* had been set down in one of the most cumbersome
systems of writing ever devised. In it, the thousands of Chinese
characters were adapted to an alien language, now to represent an
idea or thing which would be the same in both countries but have
wholly different names, and now to furnish a sound for a phonetic
representation of a Japanese syllable. Simplified versions of the
Chinese characters were gradually developed to make up a phonetic syllabary that might be used to replace Chinese characters or
to use with them, especially for representing the complex inflections
of verbs and adjectives. By and large, poetry (and certain other literary forms) came to be written in the phonetic "Japanese writing"
(*wabun*), and as men and women learned the new system, they
came to be unable to read the first great collection of their poetry.
The prefigurings of new styles in the works of poets like Yakamochi might never have been. In addition, Japanese poetry suffered in a craze for Chinese, and it must have seemed to some in
danger of becoming a plaything in amorous affairs.

Such at least is the usual view, and such the implicit regret felt
by modern Japanese as they turn from what they often call the
"*Man'yō*" to the "*Kokin*" period. There can be no doubt that there
were serious losses—of public poetry, for example—but there were
remarkable gains as well. As a whole, the period from 784 to 1100,
which may be called the early classical period, is certainly the most
original and perhaps the greatest in Japanese literature, as a brief
catalogue of major works and literary conventions may suggest. It
must be understood that all the dates are approximate (and sometimes the subject of warm disagreement), and that only representative classics or forms are included.

809 Poetry contests instituted.

905 *Kokinshū*: first ordered imperial anthology.

935 *The Tosa Diary*: the first poetic diary, the first fictional diary.

945 *The Tales of Ise*: first and greatest of the "tales of poems" (*utamonogatari*).

950 *The Tale of the Bamboo Cutter*: "the parent of all tales," first of the prose romances (*tsukurimonogatari*).

974 *The Gossamer Diary*: a poetic diary bringing emotional realism and contemporary court customs into literature.

990ff. *The Pillow Book of Sei Shōnagon*: the greatest of Heian pensées.

1004 *The Diary of Izumi Shikibu*: the finest of the poetic diaries.

1010 *The Tale of Genji*: the greatest work of Japanese literature.

1085 Popular songs, *imayō,* at their height.

Of all the important genres of pre-modern Japanese literature, only historical fiction and drama are not represented in this list, and even they had their beginnings in this period, the first in works like *The Tale of Genji,* the second in the "monkey music" (*sarugaku*) of the court. In addition, new classes of writers emerged—always associated somehow with the court—the most important being the high nobility, priests, and women. The explanation for this astonishing record of literary achievement is the fact that the early classical period was politically and socially the great age of the court. At such a time, the society itself (as distinct from its individual writers) was at its most creative.

The *Kokinshū,* or *Collection of Ancient and Modern Times,* completed about 905, set the pattern for all subsequent orderings of court collections and sequences. We may even say that the seasonal poems in the *Kokinshū* set the basic terms for *haiku* written today, and that over the centuries its vision of courtly love has illuminated for Japanese the essential experience of love. In addition, Tsurayuki's Preface initiated Japanese literary criticism, both as a literary enterprise and as a view of literature with certain fundamental preoccupations. Such versatility in devising not only new forms but also new modes of apprehension is a measure of the vigor of court society at its peak. Whatever else may be said of the hiatus between the *Man'yōshū* and the *Kokinshū*, it seems clear that the break forced poets to look upon themselves afresh and to devise a new poetry of their own poetic resources, with whatever help they might wish to accept from Chinese models.

The new poetry began to emerge in the third and fourth decades of the ninth century and was thriving by its third quarter. This was the period of the so-called Six Poetic Geniuses—the Bishop Henjō, Bunya Yasuhide, the Priest Kisen, Ōtomo Kuronushi, Ono no Komachi, and Ariwara Narihira—who earned their title by being mentioned in Tsurayuki's Preface. As in earlier and later times, the best poets were courtiers of middling rank or men and women from families whose fortunes were in decline. The Ariwara family (or "clan"), the Ono family, and the Ki family produced many of the best poets, but it was the Fujiwara family that had come to have most of the power and wealth.

The *Kokinshū* was designed to embody a tradition of Japanese poetry from a dimly conceived age of the gods, through such by then dim figures as Hitomaro, and such already legendary figures as Ariwara Narihira (825–80) and Ono no Komachi (fl. ca. 850), down to men and women who had acquired fame only yesterday. The inclusion of poems attributed to Hitomaro or Akahito, or those collected by the Bureau of Song, justified the "Ancient" in the title. The two generations best represented in the *Kokinshū*, however, are the generation of the Six Poetic Geniuses (ca. 850–65), and that of the compilers of the *Kokinshū* (ca. 900). Of the many poets included in the collection, four stand out—Komachi, Narihira, Ki no Tomonori (fl. ca. 890), and Ki no Tsurayuki (868–945). There is also an important body of anonymous poems as well as poems by one or two poets whose work appears mainly in later collections.

The poetry of Komachi is above all passionate, so much so that it alone could have created the legend of her love affairs, but it is also so technically skillful that the passion is made real. No Japanese before her had re-created in poetry the experience of what it was like to have the feverish urges to passion denied (*KKS*, XIX: 1030).

Hito ni awan	On such a night as this
Tsuki no naki ni wa	When no moon lights your way to me,
Omoiokite	I wake, my passion blazing,
Mune hashiribi ni	My breast a fire raging, exploding flame
Kokoro yakeori.	While within me my heart chars.

Paradoxically, the darkness causes the flames, and sleep yields to the greater nightmare of life. The conceit of fire is buried in no fewer than three pivot-words, giving the feeling that the language is being pressed as hard as the emotions of the woman. In one way or another, such a combination of technique and feeling is typical of the early classical period. The new poets made two discoveries: that subjective private experience could be of universal significance, and that feeling needed calculated art to convey it. The techniques employed might differ, but they were expected to have, as Tsurayuki put it, *sama,* style, and in particular a style reflecting the oblique, witty, conceited, dialectical qualities of the Chinese poetry of the Six Dynasties.

The result was in part a great concern with the "words" of poetry, and especially a tendency to employ techniques that would distinguish as finely as possible the nature of what is real from what is illusory. The full force of certain Buddhist conceptions of the illusory nature of mundane experience was now felt in Japanese poetry, and no less in the intense passion of a Komachi. She might not draw a Buddhist moral from human attachments, but she could turn Buddhist logic against the unfaithfulness of men (*KKS,* XV: 797).

Iro miede	That which fades away
Utsurou mono wa	Without revealing its altered color
Yo no naka no	Is, in the world of love,
Hito no kokoro no	That single flower which blossoms
Hana ni zo arikeru.	In the fickle heart of man.

Even in the English we sense the word association of the original and see how its sequence of fades away/color/flower develops into a metaphor. The flower is that of human love. Its fading represents the man's growing infidelity, even while the former color, or pretense to love, is maintained. The most significant word in the poem is "color" (*iro*), which conveys a complex of meanings. It refers to the fading of man's affections, to sexual passion, and—most significant of all—to appearance as opposed to the reality of man's untrustworthy heart (*kokoro*). That heart should be the essential truth, but the color it assumes falsifies it. In such fashion Komachi plays on Buddhist ideas of the illusory nature of experience and on the contrast of underlying truth. What she treats as real is, however, the falseness of man, and the essential reality of the heart turns out to be the grossest deception. What finally is implied as the truly desirable reality is realized passion, which is as little a Buddhist notion as it is a Calvinist one.

The passionate technique, or the conceited reality, of Komachi's poetry foreshadows Tsurayuki's simultaneous insistence on the spontaneous nature of poetry and on the importance of technique. What is especially individual about Komachi is that her strongest passions seem to bring forth her most complex techniques. In the end, however, nothing in her poetry matters so much as the obsessive passion behind it. Driven by this passion, she is often able to get at very significant kinds of experience that elude other poets (*KKS*, XIII: 658).

Yumeji ni wa	Although my feet
Ashi mo yasumezu	Never cease running to you
Kayoedo mo	On the path of dreams,
Utsutsu ni hitome	Such nights of love are never worth
Mishi goto wa arazu.	One glimpse of you in your reality.

As readers of *The Tale of Genji* will recall, it was believed that in dreams one's soul could leave one's body and, trailing a connecting thread or cord, could visit the person of one's passion. Komachi declares herself to be a habitual nocturnal commuter, and the admission reveals how passionately she desires to meet her lover. Yet that is not enough: she wants the reality of her lover to come to her. Dream (*yume*) and reality (*utsutsu*) are charged terms among these poets, as one can see in another of her poems (*KKS*, XIII: 656).

Utsutsu ni wa	In waking daylight,
Sa mo koso arame	Then, oh then, it can be understood;
Yume ni sae	But when I see you
Hitome o moru to	Shrinking from those hostile eyes
Miru ga wabishisa.	Even in my dreams: that is misery itself.

Fearing exposure in court gossip, she shrinks from other people even in her dreams; yet the "hostile eyes" of others (*hitome*) are nothing to her own self-conscious shame—or to the passion driving her to such self-exposure. Her dreams have become as passionate as reality itself, and the reality of her love has become a nightmare.

Komachi has poems that are more reflective and even some that are playful, but the passion is always there. Even when reflective, as in the poem of hers best known to Japanese, she posits as it were the axiom of passion (*KKS*, II: 113).

Hana no iro wa	The cherry blossoms
Utsurinikeri na	Have passed away, their color lost,
Itazura ni	While to no avail
Waga mi yo ni furu	Age takes my beauty as it falls
Nagame seshi ma ni.	In the long rain of my regret.

Out of her passion and such a poem as this came the legend of Komachi the beautiful lover who grew old, ugly, and despised. What made her such a legendary figure was, however, the intensity of her feeling, rather than the moral about growing old. To the court poets the legacy she bequeathed was less a code of love than a testament of the validity of passion. After her there was no generation of court poets in whose poetry passionate women played no part. More important, Komachi established once and for all that the driving force of courtly love—in prose and most prose fiction—was to be the woman's needs and feelings. The moralists amongst us may wonder if Komachi did not have only herself to blame for her sufferings, but Japanese poets of both sexes (unlike most Western poets) have followed her in thinking that the woman's case conveys the truth of love far better than the man's.

Narihira also became a legend as a lover in his own time. It is difficult to say which is the more remarkable—his reputed effect on every lady within reach or his ability to find profound meaning in seemingly casual affairs. (One of the most interesting of Landor's imaginary conversations would have been a meeting of Komachi and Narihira.) We can understand something of the nature of his effect on women from a poem by, of all people, the

Shrine Priestess of Ise. She wrote him after a night of love (*KKS*, XIII: 645).

Kimi ya koshi	My mind is dazzled—
Ware ya yukiken	Did you come to visit me?
Omōezu	Or I to you?
Yume ka utsutsu ka	Was our night a dream? Reality?
Nete ka samete ka?	Was I sleeping? Or was I awake?*

He had his effect on others as well. Once he visited a lady by taking advantage of a break in the earthen wall around her family's house. Thereafter, at least in fiction, a lover was apt to clamber through an earthen wall to reach his lady. Or again, his friendship with Prince Koretaka became a model of courtly *amicitia* and elegance. Yet what is remarkable about Narihira is that we discover behind the legend a man not only more credible but also more admirable than the storied lover. His reply to the Shrine Priestess is of an order of poetic greatness and insight far above hers or the legends surrounding him (*KKS*, XIII: 646).

Kakikurasu	Through the blackest shadow
Kokoro no yami ni	Of the darkness of the heart I wander
Madoiniki	In bewilderment—
Yume utsutsu to wa	You who know the world of love, decide:
Yohito sadame yo.	Is my love reality or dream?

Apart from the haunting cadences of the original, and the way in which its rhythms perfectly obey the sense, there is a quality of passionate philosophy or philosophical passion that is Narihira's own. The darkness of the heart is the Buddhist metaphor for attachment to this world, and especially for human love. He admits to being lost in such darkness, and he appeals to those who know love to tell him whether it is dream or reality. Their answer may be, as Komachi's no doubt would have been, that passionate love is the only reality we can know. But Narihira's question unmistakably implies that what was so wonderfully real when it

* The questions are not only Japanese, of course. A lesser-known eighteenth-century play, *The West Indian,* of Richard Cumberland (1771), shows a confused character who asks (II, vii): "Am I in a dream? Is this a reality?" But the compulsion to distinguish the two is particularly Japanese, particularly Buddhist.

happened is in the long view only illusion. And yet he acknowledges how human it is to adopt the short view.

The character of Narihira's poetry is difficult to convey in English, since it possesses a fine balance of certain qualities that may seem contradictory. With the passion of a Komachi he combines philosophical reflection, and with great beauty of cadence and phrase he has yet a gift for concentrated language. We may take his lament, "Composed When I Was Weak with Illness" (*KKS*, XVI: 861).

Tsui ni yuku	Though formerly I heard
Michi to wa kanete	About the road that all must travel
Kikishikado	At the inevitable end,
Kinō kyō to wa	I never thought that this today
Omowazarishi o.	Would bring that far tomorrow.

The original makes man's life seem incomparably valuable, even as its sounds and rhythms haunt us with an inexorable music of time. It has the capacity to convey more than one would think could be said in words—as later critics recognized—but it also shows that its author's greatness is, like Racine's, predicated on, and perhaps confined to, the language it makes seem so inevitably true. Thought, feeling, and language seem each to enhance the other, and a translator can only bewail his inadequacy to convey them.

Narihira's essential seriousness does not preclude light touches or glancing wit. There is a poem, for example, in which he explains to a woman he has been seeing that his reason for not visiting her recently is the strange one that he has been deeply affected by the season and his love for her (*KKS*, XIII: 616).

Oki mo sezu	I am at one with spring:
Ne mo sede yoru o	Neither sleeping, nor yet rising from
Akashite wa	my bed,
Haru no mono tote	Till night turns into dawn,
Nagamekurashitsu.	And through the day my love for you continues
	In listless looking at the ceaseless rains.

As anyone knows who has lived through the rainy season in Japan, its warm, lax, and yet oppressive atmosphere tends to induce a dreamy, hypnotic trance or reverie. The speaker in the poem is in such a state, and his mood is expressed in the pivot-word *nagame-,* the ceaseless rains. The spring rains bring the trance, and his trouble is that he has yielded too far to the season. He even says that he is a thing of spring (*Haru no mono*). Yet despite the season and its effect on him, his lady might have thought herself a cause of a different effect: if he loves her, he should visit her. What he is ultimately saying in his sly attestation of an anesthetized love is that he is so wholly in tune with the nature of things that he has lost his individual capacity to get up and go. He turns her off very gently, not being certain himself just what his motives are. This, he says, is what it is like to be part of love *and* of spring.

The poem may serve as background for Narihira's most famous poem, probably the most famous of all court poems over the centuries. The long headnote to it speaks of his affair with a lady whose departure took her away from him, and how "the following spring, when the plum blossoms were at their height and on a night when the moon was particularly fine, he thought longingly of the previous year, and, going back to the western quarter of the house where she had lived, he composed the following as he lay on the boards of the deserted room until the moon set" (*KKS,* XV: 747).

Tsuki ya aranu	This is not that moon
Haru ya mukashi no	And it cannot be this is the spring
Haru naranu	Such as the spring I knew;
Waga mi hitotsu wa	I am myself the single thing
Moto no mi ni shite.	Remaining as it ever was.

Once again man's life is shown to be caught up in the natural and yet to some degree hostile rhythm of time. The speaker seemingly asserts that a human existence which Buddhism insisted is transient is somehow more stable than natural phenomena and their laws. The poet's response brings a conviction of human feeling to bear on a differing conviction of religious truth. Man is an integral part of the natural scene, and if the moon and spring change, man certainly should as well, he being bound by the same natural laws. But whereas nature changes within a larger constancy, man's attachment to the illusory leads him to change in a contrary human deviation from the larger cyclical and steadfast reality. Narihira, of course, knows that only the misguided would protest against that nature of things which includes man. What makes the poem, for all its difficulty, so central a statement of court poetry is its open-eyed understanding of the ironic disparity between human conviction and philosophical reality, between the celebration of plum flowers, moon, and spring—none of them as close to man's heart as love—and the desolation wrought upon man by time, even though he protests his integrity.* On the strength of such poems as this, Narihira, the legendary lover, may be called an intellectual among court poets. Just as Komachi brought a passionate intensity to poetry, Narihira found the terms for understanding passionate man's dubious place in the scheme of things. His poetry succeeds because its exploitation of language respects its rules, and because its assertion of individual experience invokes the fundamental laws of a Buddhist culture.

The manner of the invocation tells us a good deal about Narihira, his age, and court poetry. To some extent, he was a poet born at an awkward time. A great period of poetry was over and was not even accessible, so complex was its system of writing. The *chōka* was not a living form, and no way had yet been found to integrate *tanka* into larger wholes. Public poetry was dead. The Ariwara family had lost ground to the Fujiwara, and Narihira himself was identified with the doomed cause of Prince Koretaka, who was barred from imperial succession by intrigue in spite of the wishes of his father, the emperor. What effect any of these conditions had on Narihira's life or on his poetry we cannot know. What is clear is that he was a great poet for whom the existing resources and conventions of poetry were insufficient.

Some later writers regarded him as a major predecessor who was yet not altogether a suitable model; Tsurayuki, for example,

---

* In view of the difficulty of translating the poem, I may add the more explanatory rendering given in *Japanese Court Poetry*.

What now is real?
This moon, this spring, are altered
     From their former being—
While this alone, my mortal body, remains
As ever changed by love beyond all change.

pithily assessed the poetic features of Narihira's dilemma by saying that his poems possessed "too much heart and too few words"
(*kokoro amarite, kotoba tarazu*). His "words" include significant
ideas and language both harmonious in sound and exact in meaning. But we sense that there is more in his poetry pressing to come
out if only it could. Like other poets of the period, Narihira strikes
us as a very different writer from Akahito. It is as though a mighty
man has somehow been fitted into a lovely woman's body. His best
poems have tinges of uneasiness, of self-doubt, of question about
his own role. And yet they are tonic; they possess not only health
but universality. The passion that drives and the thought that re-
strains together explore major themes of court poetry.

Narihira's imagery, in comparison to that of other major court
poets, is so simple that it almost seems unimportant. But closer
consideration reveals that there is usually one central image chosen
from many that are possible or implied. As the headnote to his
most famous poem shows, he might have chosen to focus on the
woman he loved (it is after all a love poem among the books of
love poems in the *Kokinshū*), on plum blossoms, on the house the
woman lived in, or on the experience of passing the night there
on the boards of the deserted room. Each of these subjects, these
images—these "words"—provided other poets with the materials
for significant poetry. But what he chose was the moon in relation
to himself. In other poems the dominant image may be rain, darkness, flood, a robe, a road, but always the crucial personal and yet
exterior image relates to the central self, to the human predica-
ment of the individual. Moreover, in the poem we are considering,
of all the images suggested by the headnote, the moon is the one
best able to express what is implied by the others, what the poet
feels to be the "heart" of the experience. As a result, the image becomes imbued with more than ordinary significance. It would be
a symbol if it were not so certainly itself.

What makes Narihira so important is that the "heart" of his
poetry reflects the profound and normative features of his culture.
When the Ise Shrine Priestess asked, rather in the conventional
dialectical language of the age, whether their night of love had
been reality or dream, he demands to know whether the spontaneous certainty of man's deepest attachments or the inexorable

Buddhist causation is, finally, more real. With a minimum of fuss, and indeed with an affirmative wit, he demonstrates that to be a "thing of spring" (*Haru no mono*) deprives him of spring's satisfactions, including love. In his most famous poem he shows that man is (though he says, as it were, more passionately, "I am") at once irretrievably cut off from nature and other men and yet inextricably bound up with them. It is often said that Buddhism insists on a fundamental nondualistic metaphysics. Narihira, however, taught Japanese poets that human experience was different from that, in involving one kind of dualism of man and nature within a larger monism subjecting both to the same laws. This paradox often provides a philosophical (indeed a universally human) basis for the dual themes of celebration and deprivation in Japanese literature. Later poets faced the same essential realities, even as they confronted a world greatly altered in the terms with which such realities presented themselves. Their problem was at once to keep, explore, and extend Narihira's understanding, devising their own terms of expression.

For the rest of the age, the terms devised were largely conventions of technique, although it was always the case that the springs of passion might unexpectedly overflow. Not many later poems in the early classical period approach the resonance of Narihira's finest work. But the age was, as we have seen, so extraordinarily inventive that it could create and bring to maturation most of the premodern forms of Japanese literature. Literary criticism, the structured anthology, and the establishment of the language of poetry—these were but three of the important literary achievements of the age. They, and others that might be mentioned, show a dominant concern with form and style (*sama*). While believing as its central article of poetic faith that poetry was natural and spontaneous to man, the age found its characteristic genius in the demonstration that poetry was precisely a civilized preoccupation —an art.

It is not surprising that such an aristocratic society should have found a value in poetic style, since it sets style as an ideal in other realms. But more attention to style inevitably meant less room for the passionate engagement so characteristic of Komachi and Narihira. Tomonori has a poem rather like Narihira's on the moon and spring, but though it has more specifiable art it has less drive (*KKS*, II: 84).

Hisakata no	On a day in spring
Hikari nodokeki	When the light throughout the sky
Haru no hi ni	Warms with tranquillity,
Shizugokoro naku	Why is it with unsettled heart
Hana no chiru ran.	That the cherry flowers fall?

There is the pillow-word "throughout the sky" (*Hisakata no*) for "light" (*Hikari*) to amplify the lovely scene, and we observe that the line *Shizugokoro naku* ("With unsettled heart") is appropriately the only one not beginning with an "h" sound; all else is settled in the harmony of spring. Such elements bespeak a careful art. In its theme, the poem resembles Narihira's: the unsettled heart is really man's; nature is after all largely constant within its smaller changes. But of course we cannot regard the poem apart from its technique, because that is what gives it a greater immediate effect than Narihira's. And yet that effect, implying such a celebration of the world, is attained at the expense of the tragic significance that Narihira discovered. Tomonori's art implies that he has not been thrown back upon his personal resources so radically—he is confident that his society and civilization will support him.

Tomonori was by no means without passion or conviction, as his love poems show (*KKS*, XII: 615; XIII: 667).

Inochi ya wa	What good is life?
Nani zo wa tsuyu no	It is really nothing more substantial
Adamono o	Than the drying dew—
Au ni shi kaeba	I would exchange it without regret
Oshikaranaku ni.	For just one night with her I love!

Shita ni nomi	It cannot be borne,
Koureba kurushi	One cannot shut love up in the heart—
Tama no o no	So let my soul-thread
Taete midaren	Break and scatter wantonly:
Hito na togame so.	Let none be shocked by what I do.

Yet there is a change from Komachi in such declarations, a new self-consciousness, a sense that the art enabling one to convey life has its own importance. For some poets of the age, or perhaps for all the poets on some occasions, the new discovery of their art meant a concern merely with technique. But the poetry reaches its finest achievement when it goes beyond technique by finding in art a truth that cannot be uncovered in life pure and simple. Another poem by Tomonori (*Kokin Rokujō* in *K. Taikei*, IX, 264) suggests as much.

Fukikureba	As it blows on me,
Mi ni mo shimikeru	The autumn wind has penetrated
Akikaze o	Through my very flesh—
Iro naki mono to	Why did I regard it as a thing
Omoikeru kana.	That lacks the color of human love?

Wind cannot penetrate the body and has, of course, no color. But the attribution to it of such properties creates a convincing truth about love. The sense of physical pain produced by the autumn wind is precisely that of this experience of love, and, by treating the wind and love in terms of the metaphor of color common to both, Tomonori fully establishes their resemblance.

Though the meaningfulness of art is the discovery of the age, it was Tsurayuki who made the discovery canonical. His concept of *sama* or style can be understood from the verses he wrote on the death of his cousin and fellow compiler of the *Kokinshū*, To-monori (*KKS*, XVI: 838).

Asu shiranu	Although I know
Waga mi to omoedo	My body is a thing with no tomorrow,
Kurenu ma no	Yet am I cast in grief
Kyō wa hito koso	In the remaining dusk of my today
Kanashikarikere.	For him already taken by the dark.

The poem has the new style partly in its rhetorical foundation on the contrast of "tomorrow" and "today." More important, it has what Japanese refer to as "reasoning." Tsurayuki's logical structure is: "Although ... / Yet ..." Another popular structure is: "Be-cause ... / Therefore ..." *Perhaps, because, since, if, so, although, seems*—these are attempts in English to translate the verb terminations relied upon for "reasoning" by poets of the early classical period.

Yet we recall once again that Tsurayuki said that all living beings are spontaneously given to song. Sometimes, indeed, the element of reasoning is slight in his work, as in this poem, "Composed When I Heard a Wood-Thrush Sing" (*KKS*, III: 160).

Samidare no	Echoing fills the sky
Sora motodoro ni	From which the summer rain is falling—
Hototogisu	And you, you wood-thrush,
Nani o ushi to ka	What anguish is it that brings you
Yo tada naku ran?	To sing uninterrupted through the night?

The polish of the original and the allusion to Chinese legends of the sufferings of the wood-thrush (resembling the Philomela legend of the nightingale) bespeak real art—but an art beating with the spontaneous pulse of life. The harmony between art and feeling is found, with a slight preponderance of one element or the other, in all the great poetry of the age. The evidence of Tsurayuki's poems in the *Kokinshū* has led Japanese scholars to conclude that he thought it most important that his generation establish the artistic basis of Japanese poetry and that he was willing to let spontaneity of feeling take second place to art. In *The Tosa Diary*, by contrast, which he wrote about thirty years after the *Kokinshū* was compiled, he emphasizes the sorrow of life more than the beauty of art. That is not to say that he ceased to be an artist in the *Diary*, or that he had not felt deeply in his earlier poems, but rather that there is a perceptible difference in emphasis. The mother mourning the death of her daughter in Tosa is a fictional creation, but the fiction itself permits a naturalness of response (*Nikki*, no. 4).

Aru mono to	I kept forgetting
Wasuretsutsu nao	That the child was dead and, asking,
Naki hito o	As if she were alive,
Izura to tou zo	"What can that girl be up to?"
Kanashikarikeru.	I have fallen into a greater grief.

Tsurayuki was at his happiest when spontaneous feeling led him to artistic expression, or, to put it more exactly, when the artistic was most natural. One of the ways in which he achieved such harmony was by creating an aura of romance, as in his poem "Composed When I Visited a Mountain Temple" (*KKS*, II: 117).

Yadori shite	I found my dwelling—
Haru no yamabe ni	It was on the hillslopes of the spring
Netaru yo wa	That I slept the night,
Yume no naka ni mo	And even in my dreams I saw
Hana zo chirikeru.	The cherry blossoms falling still.

Here, conscious experience is at one with subconscious; in this, as well as in the magical quality of the scene, Tsurayuki anticipates later poets. That was typical of him and his age—to strike off in numerous directions, boldly trying this and that posture, often without settling for long on any one.

Apart from the intrinsic quality of his work and the variety of his experimentation, Tsurayuki's importance rests on two seemingly contradictory feats that he yet managed to bring together. By his criticism and, above all, by his practice, he proved that Japanese poetry rested on artistic canons that could be taught and practiced as an art; and by precept and demonstration he also maintained the naturalness of art, the spontaneity of song. The art of his love poems does not convince us that he was a great lover, as do the poems of Narihira. But the steadiness, the self-consciousness of his experience are themselves truths conveyed in his art. The love poems therefore convince us that he writes of situations as real as those dealt with by any poet, as this winter poem suggests (*SIS*, IV: 224).

Omoikane	Pressed by yearning,
Imogariyukeba	I set out hunting for her I love,
Fuyu no yo no	And since the winter wind
Kawakaze samumi	Is cold as it blows up from the river,
Chidori naku nari.	The plovers cry out in the night.

After Tsurayuki there were a number of brilliant women who reverted to the style of intense passion introduced by Komachi. One of the first was Lady Ise (fl. ca. 900), whose dates are unclear except that she seems to be a younger contemporary of Tsurayuki. One of her poems was "Composed at a Time When I Was in Love, as I Saw the Burnt-over Fields Along the Road During a Trip" (*KKS*, XV: 791).

Fuyugare no	Because I feel
Nobe to waga mi o	My passion-wasted self like fields
Omoiseba	Withered by winter,
Moete mo haru o	Can I hope for better springtime
Matamashi mono o.	If I am burnt away like them?

The comparison of her passion to the burning of fields is extended in a conceit throughout the poem. Komachi had introduced the technique, but Ise gives it a lightness and a sense of humor that are her own. Yet her famous lightness of touch in no way diminished the passion of her writing, as we can see from a poem on the effects of night after night of love (*KKS*, XIV: 681).

Yume ni dani	Not even in dreams
Miyu to wa mieji	Dare I show my face to him henceforth:
Asana asana	Day by day my shame
Waga omokage ni	Increases as the image in my mirror
Hazuru mi nareba.	Reveals new ravages of love.

After Lady Ise, the most considerable poet to write in such a vein is Izumi Shikibu (ca. 970–1030), who, like Ise and Komachi, led a life that more proper people thought abandoned. The author of a large body of poems and, most Japanese scholars think, of *The Diary of Izumi Shikibu,* she is the most important poet of the eleventh century. She has more than one poem imploring a visit from more than one lover, among them one "Sent to Someone When I Was Ill" (*GSIS*, XIII: 763).

Arazaran	Soon to be no more—
Kono yo no hoka no	How I wish I had you by me
Omoide ni	Now, and if but once,
Ima hitotabi no	That I might take the memory
Au koto mo ga na.	With me to the world beyond!

Even more passionate is this remarkable poem, in which intimate physical touch is treated for perhaps one of the few times in an imperial anthology (*GSIS*, XIII: 755).

Kurogami no	Lying down alone,
Midarete shirazu	I am so confused in yearning for you
Uchifuseba	That I have forgot
Mazu kakiyarishi	The tangles of my long black hair,
Hito zo koishiki.	Desiring the one who stroked it clear.

Passion alone does not produce poetry, and closely examined, Izumi Shikibu's poetry reveals a sharp intelligence and an accomplished art. A poem in *The Diary of Izumi Shikibu* (*Nikki,* no. 506) is, to be sure, a love poem, but its careful artistry takes it beyond the range of simple passion.

Tamakura no	Fallen everywhere,
Sode ni mo shimo wa	The frost lies also upon the sleeve
Okikeru o	Of the pillowing arm,
Kesa uchimireba	And looking at it in the morning light,
Shirotae ni shite.	I see it white like purest hemp.

The old pillow-word for sleeves, "white hempen" (*Shirotae no*), has been skillfully associated with the frost. Lovers were said to sleep on or under their spread garments and to pillow their heads on each other's arms. In this scene, the woman thinks of her lover on a winter morning and, missing him as she does, speaks of a frost probably implying tears. What Japanese find especially attractive in the poem is the evocative phrase, "the sleeve / Of the pillowing arm" (*Tamakura no / Sode*). Nothing could better conjure the aura of courtly lovers sharing a frosty night in the shadowed intimacy of a Heian chamber.

Izumi Shikibu wrote on other subjects than love, notably nature and religion, and on both subjects she often spoke with a new voice. The seasonal poems reveal a new degree of description. Her religious poems are fresh in expressing a passionate commitment that yet admits the truth of Buddhist doctrine. In a poem "Sent to His Eminence Shōku" (*SIS,* XX: 1342), the moon symbolizes his priestly teaching.

Kuraki yori	Now I must set forth
Kuraki michi ni zo	Out of darkness on yet a darker path—
Irinu beki	O blessed moon,
Haruka ni terase	Hovering upon the mountain rim,
Yama no ha no tsuki.	Shine clearly on the way I take ahead!

She has echoed a passage in the Lotus Sûtra (VII): "Long night adds its curse to our lot: Out of darkness we enter into darkness" (trans. Arthur Waley). It may seem a matter inviting comment that the most famous religious poem of the period should have been written by a woman thought to be profligate.

The fact that a woman should write the best love and religious poetry of her time is not easily glossed by an English example. Various explanations have been advanced for the dominance of Japanese literature by women at this time. Izumi Shikibu, Murasaki Shikibu, Sei Shōnagon (author of *The Pillow Book*), the Mother of Michitsuna (author of *The Gossamer Diary*), and numerous other women made the century from about 950 to 1050 one of the greatest in the history of Japanese literature. Is there a parallel period in any other literature, not only of the preeminence of women but of the contribution by women to what is deemed classic in the nation's heritage? It seems very doubtful. Why this moment in Heian literature should be the unique instance of the phenomenon is by no means clear. The various explanations that have been offered, though sometimes profound and even persuasive, suffer from a lack of real evidence. In the circumstances, we may confine our consideration of the question to some of the anecdotes and to the speculations common to many discussions of the matter. We know that Izumi Shikibu (who may or may not have been the author of *The Diary of Izumi Shikibu*) was censured by Murasaki Shikibu (who may or may not have been the author of *The Tale of Genji,* and may or may not have been its vicarious heroine) in her own *Diary.* Izumi Shikibu was, she said, an abandoned person. She concedes, however, that Izumi Shikibu writes letters very well! Like other writers, and by no means only those of her sex, Murasaki Shikibu was unable to concede that her rival was the better poet.*

Some understanding of the efflorescence of female genius can be found in the beliefs that, if the author of the *Sarashina Diary* is typical, women were the most avid readers at the time, and that the court of Empress Akiko supported and cultivated writers. In her *Diary,* Murasaki Shikibu makes out Akiko to have been straitlaced, but it is a most remarkable form of straitlacing that led

---

* In view of their famous rivalry, one is amused to discover that in the Festival of the Ages (Jidai Matsuri) in Kyoto, the geisha representing these two great writers sit, apparently reconciled, on the same float.

her to include among her attendants not only Murasaki Shikibu and the witty, flirtatious Sei Shōnagon, but also Izumi Shikibu—after her notorious love affairs with two princes of the blood—to whom she sent a most considerate gift on the death of her daughter, Koshikibu. With Murasaki Shikibu, Akiko read Chinese on the quiet. Arthur Waley amusingly—though exaggeratedly—said that for a Heian lady to learn Chinese was roughly as daring as for the daughter of a Victorian prime minister to learn boxing. At all events, the composure required to coach an empress in Chinese poetry—not to mention the effort needed to compose so long a work as *The Tale of Genji*—took an unusual degree of energy, of motivation, almost of passion for literature. Perhaps what the female dominance of this splendid period comes down to is that it was the court ladies on whom descended one of those remarkable bursts of creative activity that so distinguish different groups in Japanese history at various times.

Something of the same thing seems to be true of Izumi Shikibu. Neither her date of birth nor her date of death is known, but the direction and drive of her life are wholly clear. She had an astonishing appetite for experience and an extraordinary capacity for passion and feeling. She loved men, her daughter, her family, and religion. She had unusual powers of discrimination and expression. We know this in a literary sense from her poetry, but the same must have been true of her personality. Two princes surely would not have fallen in love with this lady of most inconsiderable rank, one of them going so far as to treat her better than his consort, unless her strength of passion had expressed itself in that fineness of sensibility so highly prized by the age. What we know of her life may incline people at times, with Murasaki Shikibu, to censure her behavior. But what we know of her passionate devotion from her poetry leads us to understand Akiko's gesture on the death of Koshikibu.

If Murasaki Shikibu is the author of *The Tale of Genji* in anything like its present form, she is the greatest Japanese writer. If not, she is a better diarist than poet. If Izumi Shikibu is the author of *The Diary of Izumi Shikibu,* she has given an unusually successful justification of passion—that it may provide not only the most varied and profound experience open to a lady at that time but also the highest degree of awareness and discrimination. To put this another way, she combines the self-aware passion of Komachi and Narihira with Tsurayuki's commitment to art.

In addition to poems by named writers of the period, there were a number of anonymous works of high quality. Anonymity in some cases bespeaks concealment of the great; in others it suggests a gift of song bestowed on the humblest men and women that is one of the graces of the *Kokinshū*. One such poem (*KKS*, III: 139) is alluded to by later poets, perhaps for its aura of romance.

Satsuki matsu	Now that the fragrance
Hanatachibana no	Rises from the orange trees
Ka o kageba	That wait till June to bloom,
Mukashi no hito no	I am reminded of those scented sleeves
Sode no ka zo suru.	And wonder about that person of my past.

Another favorite (*KKS*, IX: 409) is lovely in its rhythms and suggestions of veiled romance.

Honobono to	Dimly, dimly
Akashi no ura no	In the morning mist that dawns
Asagiri ni	Over Akashi Bay,
Shimagakureyuku	My longings follow with the ship
Fune shi zo omou.	That vanishes behind the distant isle.

Lyrics such as these possess a purity belonging to all periods and to none. Indeed, possibly some of these anonymous poems in the *Kokinshū* date from a relatively early time; they may be in effect songs that were thought too good to forget, even during the height of the fancy for things Chinese.

Although the early classical period is dominated in its early stage by such anonymous lyrics and by the intensity of poets like Komachi and Narihira, and in its later stage by the literary supremacy of women following Izumi Shikibu, the characteristic achievement of the age is that of Tsurayuki. During the eleventh century, men of great sobriety or solemnity were bestirring themselves over his legacy, and it was natural that there should appear conservative and liberal disputants over what he had left. Half of the double legacy was his art, which was so impressive to some as to discourage any experimentation. He and his generation had set the "words" of poetry, both in the strict sense, and in the more general sense of providing materials, subjects, rhetoric, imagery, and even syntax that were recognizably poetic. That conventional or traditional half of the legacy led to the special canonical status for the first three imperial collections and to what may be called the official "Fujiwara style," a phrase implying a dominant poetic mode compounded of one part of elegance and several of convention. After the tenth century, everybody who aspired to the rank of poet had to master that amalgam of the "reasoning" style and the language of the *Kokinshū, Gosenshū,* and *Shūishū.* Even the most radical poets produced the bulk of their work in this style. With this part of his legacy, Tsurayuki had insured competence. But he did not insure greatness. Of course no conception of poetry can automatically call forth greatness, but what he also did was provide in his legacy a more liberal second half, the belief in the primacy of spontaneous feeling. But to believe that art is natural does not decree a final balance with life. There was much for later poets to adjust for themselves.

Looking back on the early classical period, we may see an age lavish to the point of prodigality in the variety of its doings. Some of its enthusiasms are annoying—for example, the seemingly pointless acrostic poems in the tenth book of the *Kokinshū.* For all that, the greatness of the period derives not only from its literary variety and critical insight, but also from the assurance of a society at the zenith of its development. It was the early classical period that laid the basis for court poetry of the next five centuries, and, *mutatis mutandis,* for traditional Japanese literature in all its forms. Tsurayuki knew the answer when he asked, "Is there any living being not given to song?" Poetry was as natural as speech or living and rose from the heart. Only it required art to "flourish in the countless leaves of words."

CHAPTER SIX

Major Poets from 1100 to 1241

The mid-classical period, that is, the age from 1100 to 1241, was not as variously inventive as the preceding period had been, in large measure because the court was now trying less to explore the possibilities of its world than to hold on against the new order of the warrior aristocracy. It sought rather to deepen than to extend, to give what had been inherited an additional richness and resonance. In this it was brilliantly successful, and its poetic achievement was the most profound in court poetry. The development of new styles and aims began in the preceding period, when a tendency toward description emerged in the poems of writers like the eccentric Sone no Yoshitada (fl. ca. 985) and the innovating Minamoto Tsunenobu (1016–97). By the time Tsunenobu's son Shunrai (?1057–1129) had compiled the fifth imperial collection, the *Kin'yōshū* (ca. 1124–27), the descriptive style was well established.

Description was significant because it was a way of giving new weight to the world—to all lying outside that subjective observer who had been the center of sensibility in the previous period. The emergence of description was a symptom of a search for a new balance between man and the world, between mind and object, and between "heart" and "words." But merely to describe was not the aim for long. The simple declarative verse to be found scattered through the *Man'yōshū* was not possible for men and women nurtured in the tradition of Tsurayuki. The world described had, after all, to have significance for man as he looked on it. Fujiwara Shunzei (1114–1204), the great arbiter of poetry in his day, put the matter forcefully, if rather vaguely. A poem, he wrote,

> should somehow ... produce an effect both of charm and of mystery and depth. If it is a good poem, it will possess a kind of

atmosphere distinct from its words and their configuration and
yet accompanying them.*

Being Japanese, Shunzei often illustrated such general points as
these with examples from earlier poets; Narihira's poem on the
changed moon and spring was one he admired greatly. Our problem is, however, to understand what Shunzei meant by "charm"
(*en*) and "mystery and depth" (*yūgen*). The terms have proved
elliptical and elusive, both in any given usage and in their development. Even the unusually complex mind of Kamo no Chōmei
(1153–1216) was nonplussed by what *yūgen* meant. His teacher,
the Priest Shun'e (fl. ca. 1160–80), gave a lengthy answer to the
direct question from Chōmei; after various evasions and examples,
Shun'e settled on an explanation paraphrasing in its climax Tsurayuki's Preface to the *Kokinshū*.

It is only when many meanings are compressed into a single
word, when the depths of feeling are exhausted yet not expressed, when an unseen world hovers in the atmosphere of the
poem, when the mean and common are used to express the elegant, when a poetic conception of rare beauty is developed to
the fullest extent in a style of surface simplicity—only then, when
the conception is exalted to the highest degree and "the words
are too few," will the poem, by expressing one's feelings in this
way, have the power of moving Heaven and Earth within the
brief confines of thirty-one syllables and be capable of softening
the hearts of gods and demons.†

The debt to Tsurayuki has been repaid by a new conception.
Rather than a poetry in which explicit analysis and synthesis was
the rule, as in much of the early classical period, he advocates a
poetry whose immediate surfaces are important only for what they
imply of greater depths.

The alternative style of charm (*en*) is one more readily understood in the work of the generation after Shunzei. His son Teika
(1162–1241) practiced in his earlier years a style referred to as that
of "ethereal beauty" (*yōembi*), and numerous writers followed

* Shunzei, *Jichin Oshō Jikaawase* in *NKGT*, II, 358.
† Chōmei, *Mumyōshō, NKGT*, III, 313.

his lead. The styles of charm or ethereal beauty offered means of heightening the attractiveness of what was dealt with and provided a way of adjusting the urge to celebration in Japanese poetry to a new end. A poem by Teika is often given as an instance of the ideal of ethereal beauty. Writing on "The Imperial Banquet of the New Year" (*Shūi Gusō* in *K. Taikei*, XI, 389), Teika might have been expected to evoke images of the palace or of auspicious pines. He gave instead:

Haru kureba	As spring comes
Hoshi no kurai ni	And the stars in the firmament
Kage miete	Shed their ranks of light,
Kumoi no hashi ni	At the edge of the cloud kingdom
Izuru taoyame.	Appear bright maidens of the stars.

The allegory of stars for courtiers and star maidens for ladies is at once understandable and unusual for a congratulatory poem, but it is above all the aura of magic that is characteristic of the style of charm.

As the styles of charm and ethereal beauty celebrated beauty, the *yūgen* style concerned itself with that desolation that has always brought out the deepest in Japanese feeling. What came to be prized was an experience for which the Japanese gave another untranslatable word, *sabi*, which is usually rendered "loneliness" or "melancholy." It was commonly associated with nature and especially with humble scenes—withered reeds, a drab bird, or huts clustered in the autumn dusk. What is implied is the absence or loss of the usual appeal, a deprivation or loss in the heart that yet suggests great beauty. Some recent Japanese critics have emphasized the Buddhist elements in such ideals along with the feeling of terror that poets often held suspended within restrained beauty. The court poet best loved by Japanese, the Priest Saigyō (1118–90), conveyed *sabi* and *yūgen* perfectly in a poem explicitly religious (*SKKS*, IV: 362).

Kokoro naki	While denying his heart,
Mi ni mo aware wa	Even a priest cannot but know
Shirarekeri	The depths of a sad beauty:
Shigi tatsu sawa no	From the marsh a longbill
Aki no yūgure.	Flies off in the autumn dusk.

So humble a bird is beautiful, and yet attachment even to one's child risks one's salvation. Man is caught, justly loving even the most pathetic things, losing his chances for a better afterlife by attaching importance to what is so slight. Yet the slight and humble can be truly attractive, and the poet's dilemma is that he knows and feels the contradiction.

Two other poems typical of the age will illustrate the paradox. The first, by Emperor Go-Toba (1180–1239), takes its departure from the opening section of Sei Shōnagon's *Pillow Book* (*Makura no Sōshi*), where she specified the ideal of certain kinds of natural beauty, associating, for example, the dawn with spring and the evening with autumn. Go-Toba's topic was "A Spring View of One's Village by the Waterside" (*SKKS*, I: 36).

Miwataseba	As I look about,
Yamamoto kasumu	Where spring haze drifts below the hills
Minasegawa	Along Minase River,
Yūbe wa aki to	I wonder what could have made me think
Nani omoiken.	That autumn was the only time for dusk?

Haze is traditionally the dominant image for spring, and Go-Toba has used it to create a monochromatic scene suggestive of the loveliest of faint coloring. It is consciously beautiful, but he knows that in praising this moment of the season he goes against tradition. A soul-piercing, sombre beauty is the quality thought quintessentially characteristic of autumn dusk, but even in spring the ideal is seen by Go-Toba as one of unquestionable beauty. Fujiwara Teika writes a poem in the opposite vein—one of the three famous poems on autumn dusk in the *Shinkokinshū* (IV: 363).

Miwataseba	As I look about,
Hana mo momiji mo	What need is there for cherry flowers
Nakarikeri	Or crimson leaves?
Ura no tomaya no	The inlet with its grass-thatched huts
Aki no yūgure.	Clustered in the growing autumn dusk.

The poem is basically more orthodox in its preferences than is Go-Toba's. For all that, we see that the beauty has been discovered in what is most humble. Go-Toba had, after all, a palace at Minase, but Teika's vision is of poor huts. More than that, their beauty, and the satisfaction of the gazer, are near extinction as darkness and winter come. To interpret such a theme in terms of the symbolism of death would be somewhat too Western for Teika's poem. Rather there is a powerful sense of the precarious nature of existence (*sonzai*) in a world beautiful and yet as transient (*hakanaki*) as the moment before autumn night. There is no grisly *Danse Macabre,* but there is the weight of karma (*sukuse*) and the Law (*nori*). Go-Toba's poem suggests how strong the attachment to existence and the world is—it tells us how important all of us, Buddhist or not, know our world to be. Teika's poem tells us how little time we have for such attachments before the dark. But the threat makes even the drab precious. Much that is most characteristic of Japanese literature will be found in these poems by Saigyō, Go-Toba, and Teika—the sense of the imminent loss of what is precious or the conviction that what is valuable may be found in what is on the verge of extinction.

In the preceding period, fundamental decisions had been reached about the areas of life most appropriate for poetic treatment and about the artistic means most suited for poetic exploration. It is, of course, never possible for one age to decree the terms of poetry for their successors. (In fact, when it was assumed by some of the heirs of Shunzei and Teika that their illustrious ancestors had given all the answers, poetry was in danger of suffocation by its conventions.) Nonetheless, early writers often pose the problems that remain crucial to a culture, and we must understand that mid-classical poets recognized the problems their predecessors had raised and that, if they were not now able to solve them, they stated them with a new profundity. In his important treatise on the aesthetic philosophy of the tea ceremony, *Nambōroku,* Sen no Rikyū (1521–91), the greatest master of the tea ceremony, gave Teika's poem (*SKKS,* IV: 363) as an expression of the Buddhist doctrine of the Void, or unreality of phenomenal things, and a symbol of the tea ceremony. Many Japanese today would say that Saigyō's poem, beginning "While denying his heart" (*Kokoro naki*), is a better example. Saigyō is important (apart from the intrinsic appeal of his poems) in that he forecasts some of the main aesthetic preferences in later poetic forms, especially in *haikai* and *haiku*. The deliberately humble image of a longbill is found to have unusual significance. If the Western reader is reminded of Wordsworth by this, the Japanese would no doubt think of Matsuo

Bashō (1644–94), the great *haikai* poet. What Saigyō's poem succeeds in doing is to convey a beauty that is incomparable because it is won from what is not lovely, and a deprivation that is felt the more fully because the awareness of loss is heightened by a precious beauty.

> Shigi tatsu sawa no   From the marsh a longbill
> Aki no yūgure.   Flies off in the autumn dusk.

Certainly by the time of Narihira court poets had that vision of man in nature which called for celebration and a sense of imminent loss. If we remember Narihira's poem on the changed moon, we can see that Saigyō has, as it were, changed Narihira's spring to autumn, his moon to a bird, his viewing place from a house to a marsh, and his subject from love to autumn. The change intensifies the privacy of the experience—we have moved from the scene of a house to almost total solitude—isolating the speaker much more and bringing the natural world into greater prominence. Because of the emphasis of his poetry, Saigyō appealed very much to Bashō, whose *Narrow Road Through the Provinces* (*Oku no Hosomichi*) alludes more often to Saigyō than to any other poet. Saigyō's poetry also spoke to modern Japanese seeking a way to harmonize Western Romantic and post-Romantic assumptions with what was yet genuinely Japanese.

This poem by Saigyō is, however, less descriptive of nature than it is subjective, existential, and, in a word, religious. It is remarkable that the first three lines have no real imagery and yet can be felt so strongly.

> Kokoro naki   While denying his heart,
> Mi ni mo aware wa   Even a priest cannot but know
> Shirarekeri . . .   The depths of a sad beauty . . .

The translation offers perhaps an unnecessarily roundabout rendering of Saigyō's Japanese, which more nearly says: "*Aware* is experienced even by one without a heart." That is, Japanese Buddhism formally required one to give up the illusions of this world in order to gain the eternal reality; this sacrifice by a priest or other devout person was said to leave him with no heart for the things of this world. The opening lines of the poem convey the dilemma in subjective, human terms, as the closing lines do in sensuous, natural terms. The beginning suggests tragedy, as the priest is drawn back to the lovely but illusory phenomenal world; the end gives something like consolation in the fact that even such a humble sight, which seems almost an aesthetic and human void, affords such beauty and significance. And yet in the balance of the two parts and in the countercurrents within each there is the creative polarity that I have termed celebration and desolation. Beauty is found at the very abyss of human darkness, and yet even the humblest scenes of the illusory world touch the ascetic heart to its depths with mingled suffering and affirmation.

In a sense, Saigyō's is a romantic version of this complex theme. Teika's version is, however, the more classical for summing up much of what was essential in earlier Japanese literature. It seems no accident that, in spite of his poor calligraphy (because of trouble with his hands), it was he who set down the most famous classics of earlier times. It is also appropriate that in his writing there should be less of the subject, of the speaker, who announces himself only in the verb of the first line, "As I look about" (*Miwataseba*). In fact, unlike Saigyō, Teika shows an obvious consciousness of other men and their lives: "The inlet with its grass-thatched huts" (*Ura no tomaya*). He was aware of other times (spring with its flowers, autumn with its leaves) and other places (famous for the leaves not at this inlet). His world is larger, more complex, and also more sublime, because by saying that there are no cherry flowers or colored leaves in the scene before him he yet manages to bring them into our experience of the poem, just as Narihira does by saying, "This is not that moon" (*Tsuki ya aranu*), or as Hitomaro evokes the presence of his wife by saying she stands forever hidden by the curtain of leaves.

The artistic heritage of Tsurayuki assured Teika of a classical composure. But as Rikyū recognized, the composure was but an aesthetic means of conveying the Void; Teika's sequence of the observer, Japanese symbolic elements (leaves and flowers), humanity (huts), and time demonstrate studied artistry. There is not the stark contrast needing to be harmonized that we find in Saigyō's poem, but rather many harmonious elements suggestive of a profound dissidence.

Regarded together, the poems suggest great differences in approach, theme, and temperament. But when the two are seen in comparison with poems of other periods, we see that they share certain characteristics—a solitary observer, a natural scene, a consciousness of irresistible attraction to even the most humble things in this illusory world, and a conviction of an inevitable void or darkness beyond. One cannot but recall those other observers of the natural scene in the best poems of Akahito and Narihira. Akahito observed, but he was withdrawn; Narihira found himself so immersed in his world that he could not, perhaps would not, extricate himself from it. Saigyō's *Kokoro naki,* without a heart, could not apply to Narihira; his problem was, as Tsurayuki might have paraphrased Saigyō, that he was *kotoba naki,* without words. Saigyō and Teika alike advanced Narihira less in basic understanding than in their capacity for expression. We may well think, therefore, that the poetic tradition had reached its ultimate achievement when poets became able for the first time (since Hitomaro) to command the means to express again and again their deepest concerns. It is, in fact, its profundity or resonance that distinguishes the poetry of this age.

Shunzei's definition of the poetic ideals of mystery and depth (*yūgen*) and charm (*en*) made possible the literary assurance of the age and the resonance that was one of its characteristics. Shunzei and Saigyō, themselves great poets and extremely attractive personalities, preceded a remarkable generation. The achievements of the older and younger generations combined to make the last years of the twelfth and the first few decades of the thirteenth century the greatest time for poetry in Japanese history. Shunzei, like Go-Toba later, could find beauty in a rare moment (*SKKS,* III: 202).

Ame sosogu	A stir of breeze
Hanatachibana ni	Touches the fragrant orange blossoms
Kaze sugite	Glistening with rain,
Yamahototogisu	And the first song of the wood-thrush
Kumo ni naku nari.	Floats in clouds among the hills.

Each of our senses is touched by the images in this style of charm (*en*), and since the bird is singing its much-awaited first song, the moment is one of great beauty. But by the same token, it is only a moment that will pass. In another poem, written "After the Death

of Teika's Mother," that is, of a wife of his own, Shunzei emphasizes the sombre sides of *yūgen*. The scene is at the woman's grave.

Mare ni kuru	I come here seldom,
Yowa mo kanashiki	But I know how sad at midnight
Matsukaze o	The wind sounds in the pines;
Taezu ya koke no	Must she listen to it forever
Shita ni kiku ran.	As she lies here underneath the moss?

The poem (*SKKS*, VIII: 796) is founded rhetorically on a contrast
between the rareness of his visits and the timelessness of her state,
a device in itself indebted to the preceding period. But the traditional contrast is given new depth by the pervasive darkness, cold,
and anguish. The conception, common to elegiac poetry the world
over, of the dead person being at once grievously dead and yet
alive to hear the disheartening wind is very well handled here.

Sometimes Shunzei wrote poems that seem better than anyone
else's to illustrate both aspects of his critical prescription of "old
words, new heart." These poems have a ripeness and inevitability
of language, imagery, and makeup that seem to have grown from
all that is true in Japanese poetry; and yet they are at the same
time works of great originality. To write poetry that was traditional and yet individual, new without being merely novel, and
inevitable but fresh—these were the high aims that Shunzei set
himself. One poem realizing the ideal was given in the second
chapter as an illustration of allusive variation on a poetic exchange
between Narihira and an unknown lady (*SZS*, IV: 258).

Yū sareba	As evening falls,
Nobe no akikaze	From along the moors the autumn wind
Mi ni shimite	Blows chill into the heart,
Uzura naku nari	And the quails raise their plaintive cry
Fukakusa no sato.	In the deep grass of Fukakusa village.

Another is an autumn poem suggestive of travel (*SKKS*, IV: 291).

Fushimiyama	Upon Fushimi Hill,
Matsu no kage yori	From this dark shelter of the pines
Miwataseba	I look across the plain,
Akuru tanomo ni	Where in the dawn the ripening fields
Akikaze zo fuku.	Softly ripple in the autumn wind.

The deep meaning and experience in the first poem is handled with complete naturalness. The perfection of the scene described in the second provides the basis for our response: there is the intimate cover from which one may look out; there are the pines, suggestive to Japanese of felicity; and there is the gradual dawning of the new day. And yet the resonance of associated words—between the "dawn" and the "lying down" and "seeing" literally suggested in *Fushi-mi*—suggests not only travel but also the brief dreams and suffering of travel. The fields are those of the harvest, the wind that of autumn and the end of things. A precious beauty and a grievous loss exist together, harmonized and convincing.

Shunzei's best poems grew from religiously disciplined exercise of his faculties. When he sat up late at night, reciting poetry in tears, he was no doubt exhibiting Japanese sensibility. But he believed in searching for the essential features (*hon'i*) of experience, and in the search he employed the "concentration and insight" (*shikan*) of Tendai Buddhism. The discipline is implied by a poem with a complex topic, "On the Spirit of Searching from Afar for the Cherry Blossoms in the Mountains" (*SCSS*, I: 57).

Omokage ni	Sending on ahead
Hana no sugata o	My contemplated image of the form
Sakidatete	Of remembered cherry flowers,
Ikue koekinu	How many ranges have I vainly crossed
Mine no shirakumo?	Taking for blossoms white clouds upon the peaks?

The "spirit" or "heart" (*kokoro*) of the search distinguishes the essence of the experience from the mere activity in a manner similar to the distinctions between reality and dream among the earlier poets. But the search is for what is essentially beautiful, for what is essentially cherry blossoms about cherry blossoms. The serious effort to arrive at truth, both traditional and new, universal and fresh, constituted Shunzei's heritage to his age. His court rank—Chamberlain to the Empress Dowager—was pitiably low, but his agreeable habit of seeing the best in all styles, whether conservative or liberal, and of emphasizing virtues rather than faults alone, made him a highly popular judge of poetry matches and sequences.

His popularity in turn gave him the opportunity to teach his ideals to his age.

Among those who appealed for advice to Shunzei was his great friend, the Priest Saigyō, who no doubt represents to Japanese what they mean by *sabi* as practiced by court poets. In his personal collection, the *Sankashū* (*K. Taikei,* XI, 255), Saigyō gave a typical expression of his feeling.

Tou hito mo	I hope no more
Omoitaetaru	That any friend will come to visit
Yamazato no	This village in the hills,
Sabishisa nakuba	And if it were not for loneliness,
Sumiukaramashi.	This would be a wretched place to live.

The love of solitude is a sophisticated attitude. Poetic expression of the idea developed in Japan from poems included in the fourth imperial collection, the *Goshūishū* (1086), though Shunzei was apparently the first to use *sabi* as a term of praise in a judgment at a poetry match in 1172. What makes Saigyō beloved by Japanese is not the sophistication of his preferences, which they largely ignore, but the simplicity and evident sincerity with which he speaks of such preferences. A Western observer of those poems of Saigyō that are highly conventional or are mannered treatments of such subjects as a passionate woman's love may have some doubt about the spontaneity of this famous priest. But there can be no question of the integrity of his life or of the mark he made on generations of Japanese, who are best able to distinguish the true from the false in their own culture. In a lovely temple in Ōhara north of Kyoto there is a cherry tree called Saigyōzakura. No one explains how it came to be called that, but it seems the finer for bearing his name.*

Saigyō's best poems are descriptive, and their description possesses that indirect symbolic relevance for man that deepens mid-classical poetry. His poem on crickets is a good example (*SKKS,* V:472).

---

*In his *Narrow Road Through the Provinces* (*Oku no Hosomichi*), Matsuo Bashō records his seeing a more famous tree of that name at Kisa Bay. Perhaps the *nō* play *Saigyōzakura* and the fact of Saigyō's wanderings led to such designations.

Kirigirisu	The crickets cry:
Yosamu ni aki no	With the quelling cold of night
Naru mama ni	Autumn hastens on,
Yowaru ka koe no	And gradually they seem to falter,
Tōzakariyuku.	The voices traveling away.

Go-Toba showed he understood the human implications in the
crickets' plight when, in his final arrangement of the *Shinkokinshū*, he placed before this poem two of his own on human anguish
in autumn. Sometimes the symbolic implications of description are
not always apparent, but there are very many clearcut cases of symbolic significance residing in apparently plain description. Saigyō
writes on a winter scene (*SKKS*, VI: 625).

Tsu no kuni no	Only a dream!
Naniwa no haru wa	The bygone glories of the spring
Yume nare ya	At Naniwa in Tsu—
Ashi no kareba ni	Everywhere the rough wind rustles over
Kaze wataru nari.	The frost-withered leaves of reeds.

The full implications of the poem require recollection of Saigyō's
allusion to a poem (*GSIS*, I: 43) written more than a century earlier by the Priest Nōin (998–1050).

Kokoro aran	If I could only show it
Hito ni miseba ya	To some one with sufficient feeling—
Tsu no kuni no	Here in Tsu Province
Naniwa watari no	The vicinity of Naniwa
Haru no keshiki o.	Is filled with sights of spring.

Spring has yielded to winter, the haze and trees in flower have
turned to reeds killed by frost. The desolation is complete, and
human hopes are dashed. It is true that Saigyō retains, partly
through allusion and partly through *sabi* and *yūgen*, a sense that
even those poor frost-wasted reeds have a precious beauty. The
beauty remains marginal, if real, even while the sense of obliter-
ating natural forces in life seems overwhelming.

The generation of Shunzei and Saigyō was followed by another
in which about ten really gifted poets emerged. The first among
this distinguished group was without question Shunzei's son Teika

(1162–1241). Long-lived like his father, Teika seemed not to have the same equable, gentle temperament. The fact that his diaries and other writings have been preserved in great detail means that we know him better as a man—warts and all—than we do other court poets. It is typical of the strength of feeling in him that he should once nearly have forfeited his chances at court by striking a superior with a lamp, and he was not above some questionable intrigue. Still, we must accord him his place as one of the greatest poets of the court. If he has not the complex humanity of Hitomaro or the combination of natural passion and philosophical reflection of Narihira, his canon of really striking poems exceeds that of either, and he was in addition a first-rate critic, scholar, anthologizer, and teacher. Moreover, he wrote in not one but several distinct styles—which is to say he created several distinct worlds—the earliest one being that of ethereal beauty, with which he captured the attention and talent of his sympathetic contemporaries. He evolved that style in a sense by asking the same sort of question as his father but by returning a different answer. Both searched for the "essences" (*hon'i*) of their subjects, and both were interested more in the "spirit" of travel or autumn than in the superficies. One of his poems, from a hundred-poem sequence on the moon, is included among the autumn poems of the *Shinkokinshū* (IV: 420).

Samushiro ya	On her straw-mat bedding
Matsu yo no aki no	The Lady of the Bridge of Uji
Kaze fukete	Spreads the moonlight out,
Tsuki o katashiku	And in the waiting autumn night
Uji no hashihime.	She lies there in the darkening wind.

In the anonymous poem alluded to (*KKS,* XIV: 689), the lover takes pleasure in imagining his beloved to be the goddess of the Uji Bridge, for even if she has to spread out a humble straw mat, she is his—at once faithful and dear. Teika's lady is less of a goddess but even more ethereal. She spreads out the moonlight, not a mat, on the boards of her dwelling. It is not so much she who waits, as in the earlier poem, but the night; and it is not the night that grows dark, but the wind. Only by following his father's prescription of "old words" is Teika able to keep his conception from becoming eccentricity or mere novelty. But it is also important that his style of ethereal beauty could contain, as in this poem, overtones of *sabi* and *yūgen* as well. The essential character of an autumn moon turns out to be a woman waiting in vain for a lover while lying sleepless on the moonlight as night waits and the wind darkens.

An even richer poem in the style of ethereal beauty is an elliptical one about spring, composed when Teika was thirty-two (*SKKS*, I: 38).

Haru no yo no	The bridge of dreams
Yume no ukihashi	Floating on the brief spring night
Todae shite	Soon breaks off;
Mine ni wakaruru	And from the mountaintop a cloud
Yokogumo no sora.	Takes leave into the open sky.

Spring nights were proverbially brief; a dream on such a night suggests on the one hand love, and on the other the fall of the mighty: in the majestic opening words of *The Tale of the Heike*, "The proud ones last but a little while; they are like a dream on a night of spring." The open sky of the poem represents the Buddhist concept of the "Void" or "Emptiness" (*kū, sora*) to which we awaken only when enlightenment ends the illusory dream of the phenomenal world. Motifs of this kind are harmonized in large measure by the dominant allusion of the poem. "The Floating Bridge of Dreams" is the title of the last chapter in *The Tale of Genji*, and Teika's echo of it suggests both the aura of courtly romance created by that beautiful story of radiant Prince Genji and his descendants and the stern workings of the Law midst the illusions in which those who follow Genji lose themselves. What poems like this require of us is an ability to apprehend fully and to experience together the value of the beautiful and the certainty of human loss.

In some other poems, Teika was more exclusively descriptive, like others of his time. His poem "Composed as a Travel Poem" (*SKKS*, X: 953) is so typical that it might have been written by any of half a dozen of his contemporaries.

Tabibito no	The traveler goes on,
Sode fukikaesu	His sleeves blowing back and forth
Akikaze ni	With the autumn wind,
Yūhi sabishiki	And the evening sun sheds lonely light
Yama no kakehashi.	Upon the bridge suspended between the cliffs.

The image of man caught in a moment in the physical sway of the bridge and in the metaphysical sway of the autumn wind on a dying day is heightened by the fact of travel away from the capital, by the reduction of the man to his sleeves, and by the emphatic word "lonely" (*sabishiki*) applied to the rays of the dying sun. The scene has a beauty, but it is the image of the man that we cannot easily forget. Another poem, which we have seen among a sequence of winter poems from the *Shinkokinshū* (VI: 671), is equally descriptive, but its winter scene is painted in a shading like that of an inkwash painting.

Koma tomete	There is no shelter
Sode uchiharau	Where I can rest my weary horse
Kage mo nashi	And brush my laden sleeves:
Sano no watari no	The Sano ford and its adjoining fields
Yuki no yūgure.	Spread over with a twilight in the snow.

Teika alludes here to a poem in the *Man'yōshū* (III: 265) in which rain and no shelter had caused distress at the same location. Now the very location of Sano is uncertain, and no shelter of any kind exists. The traveler is held as the snow falls ever deeper, and the faintly colored light of the winter dusk fades. The austere combination of deprivation and beauty is very like that in many *nō* plays, and it is no accident that this poem is echoed in the play *The Potted Tree* (*Hachi no Ki*).

Although, as Teika put it, "the springs of poetry" ran dry with his father's death, he gradually evolved another major style—that of intense feeling, or of conviction of feeling (*ushin*, or *kokoro ari*, possessing "heart"). "Whatever the style may be," he wrote in his later years, "it must possess conviction of feeling," and though this was true of all the styles he identified, it was absolutely the case with the one he designated as the style of intense feeling.* Often the later poems are simpler in language and less involved in conception. At the age of seventy, he could express with a kind of imaginative candor the feelings of a young woman just embarked upon the certainly disastrous course of courtly love (*Shūi Gusō* in *K. Taikei,* XI, 452).

Hajime yori	From long ago
Au wa wakare to	I had heard that to meet in love
Kikinagara	Could only mean to part,
Akatsuki shirade	And yet I gave myself to you
Hito o koikeri.	Unconscious of the coming dawn.

In such poems, the essential nature (*hon'i*) of the experience is approached directly, but for the woman there are subtle waves of feeling and experience in the contrast of her night and dawn. In another late poem (*Shūi Gusō* in *K. Taikei,* XI, 450), the more complex technique shows that what Teika sought with his ideal of intense feeling was an approach, whether simple or complex, that best conveyed experience.

Shitaogi mo	Rising, lying, waiting,
Okifushimachi no	Endlessly in the color of the moon,
Tsuki no iro ni	The lower reeds and I
Mi o fukishioru	Are drenched through to the lonely core
Toko no akikaze.	By the autumn wind blowing on my bed.

That the speaker is a betrayed woman is evident, but no one before Teika was likely to consider her experience of misery essential to his topic—"The Moon." "Color" (*iro*) probably has implications of love, and *okifushimachi* has a number of meanings: as three verbs, *oki* means "rising" or "waking," *fushi* "lying down," and *machi* "waiting"; *okifushi* means "endlessly" or "repeatedly." It is not now the simple, passionate being of a woman just embarked on love that Teika chooses to speak of, but the far more complex awareness of a woman having gone through the whole experience —and it is this totality that Teika uses to define the meaning of his topic, the moon. What Teika created as a personal poetic ethos was

* Teika, *Maigetsushō, NKGT,* III, 348.

a world in which incomparable human and natural beauty harmonized with the deepest sense of violated heart.

Many fine poets followed the ideals of Shunzei and Teika. A poem by the Priest Jakuren (d. 1201), generally considered his best, is one of the three famous evening poems of the *Shinkokinshū* (IV: 361). It shows how central the ideals of *sabi* and *yūgen* were to numerous poets of the age.

Sabishisa wa	Loneliness—
Sono iro to shi mo	The essential color of a beauty
Nakarikeri	Not to be defined:
Maki tatsu yama no	Over the dark evergreens, the dusk
Aki no yūgure.	That gathers on far autumn hills.

A poem by Fujiwara Ietaka (1158–1237), who risked much in his loyalty to Go-Toba, suggests the way a new heart might inform old words (*SKKS*, I: 45).

Ume ga ka ni	The plum in flower,
Mukashi o toeba	Its fragrance makes me ask about the past,
Haru no tsuki	But the soft spring moon
Kotaenu kage zo	Beams unchanged with enigmatic radiance
Sode ni utsureru.	And glistens with a sadness on my sleeve.

The "new heart" involves partly the discovery of such melancholy in spring—the moon shining in the tears on his sleeve—and partly the freshness of the spring scene. The "old words" come from the general stock of Tsurayuki's creation and involve an allusion to Narihira's poem on the changed moon and spring.

In this attempt to characterize major poets by a single poem, we ought not to overlook Kamo no Chōmei (1153–1216). A few years older than Teika, he was distinguished for his prose as well as his poetry. The unusual difficulty of his poetic style forecasts in some respects the love poems of the late classical period and the linked poetry of *renga*. Here is a relatively simple example (*SKKS*, X: 964) transliterated and paraphrased:

Makura tote	As a pillow
Izure no kusa ni	with grasses from where
Chigiru ran	will I form a bond?
Yuku o kagiri no	The place I stop is destination's
Nobe no yūgure.	evening on the moors.

Or, translated more fully:

> Where are the grasses
> That I am fated to bind up
> For a traveller's pillow?
> Any stopping-point is destination
> Upon the moors as evening falls.

The three chief poets to be mentioned after Teika are, however, Princess Shokushi (d. 1201), a woman called Shunzei's Daughter (fl. ca. 1200), and Fujiwara Ariie (1155–1216). Princess Shokushi may have been the better poet of the two women, but both were excellent and both were influenced by Teika's style of ethereal beauty blended with the style of the passionate woman, begun three and a half centuries before by Komachi. The poetry of Shunzei's Daughter is rather more like Teika's; Princess Shokushi shows stronger signs of following Komachi, as her best known poem shows. It concerns "Hidden Love" (*SKKS*, XI: 1034).

Tama no o yo	O cord of life!
Taenaba taene	Threading through the jewel of my soul,
Nagaraeba	If you break, break now:
Shinoburu koto no	My strength will go if this continues,
Yowari mo zo suru.	Unable to bear such fearful strain.

A poem of similar force but different imagery describes what it is like to have entered into the uncertainties of a love affair (*SKKS*, XI: 1074).

Shirube se yo	Guide me on my way—
Ato naki nami ni	My boat rows on across a sea
Kogu fune no	Of trackless waves,
Yukue mo shiranu	And I cannot tell where I am bound—
Yae no shiokaze.	O wind that blows up on all sides!

The aura of ethereal beauty is apt to emerge more strongly in her poems with religious overtones, as in this on a late spring scene (*SKKS*, II: 149).

Hana wa chiri	The cherry petals gone,
Sono iro to naku	There is no special color to my thoughts,
Nagamureba	Yet as I gaze,
Munashiki sora ni	From the vacant sky there falls
Harusame zo furu.	The quiet sadness of spring rain.

We have seen that the image of the vacant sky is a Buddhist metaphor for the Void, and Princess Shokushi adapts it to convey the
consciousness of her speaker. The paradox of rain falling from a
sky without clouds, like the colorless reflection upon cherry blossoms, conveys the loss of beauty felt as she muses on the scene.
So strong is the feeling that the actual physical reality becomes
illusory even while it is treated as fact. Another poem in such a
vein shows a mind divided between religion and love (*SKKS*,
XVIII: 1810).

Akatsuki no	The cock has crowed,
Yūtsukedori zo	Announcing the coming of the dawn,
Aware naru	And cries some hope
Nagaki neburi o	To a pillow sleepless in its longings
Omou makura ni.	Through the long dreams of vain desires.

A pillow with longings is very much in Teika's ethereal style, and
the Buddhist thought underlying "the long dream of vain desires"
shows how conscious the woman is that her longings are religiously perverse. Such consciousness and blending of the ethereal
and the passionate characterize the poetry of Princess Shokushi.

Shunzei's Daughter has more than a little of Teika's magic in
creating atmosphere. Alluding to an anonymous poem in the *Kokinshū* (III: 139) that we saw toward the end of the last chapter—

Satsuki matsu	Now that the fragrance
Hanatachibana no	Rises from the orange trees
Ka o kageba	That wait for June to bloom,
Mukashi no hito no	I am reminded of those scented sleeves
Sode no ka zo suru.	And wonder about that person of my past.

—she rendered an already subjective experience yet more mysterious by translating it into dream (*SKKS*, III: 245).

Tachibana no	A moment's doze
Niou atari no	Within the circle of the scent
Utatane wa	Of the orange flowers—
Yume mo mukashi no	Even in dreams the fragrance stirs my heart
Sode no ka zo suru.	To recall his scented sleeves of long ago.

In her hands, a poem on an "Evening During Travel" has, for all its tone of *sabi*, a deeper dye of tenderness than is common in the age (*SKKS*, X: 957).

Furusato mo	My only message
Aki wa yūbe o	Is the evening given me by autumn
Katami nite	From my distant home,
Kaze nomi okuru	Brought by the wind as I make my way
Ono no shinohara.	Across this plain of small bamboos.

Like Princess Shokushi, Shunzei's Daughter often wove a tight texture of language, and not the least when the feeling she expressed was strongest—in this, too, they resembled Komachi—as in a poem on the misery of the betrayed woman (*SKKS*, XIV: 1335).

Kayoikoshi	Withered, all withered,
Yado no michishiba	The grasses by the path he took to me,
Karegare ni	And rarer, yet rarer
Ato naki shimo no	Visits no longer leaving footprints
Musubōretsutsu.	As frost grips all my house and me.

A spring poem has the same texture with a very different tone (*SKKS*, II: 112).

Kaze kayou	Brought by the breeze,
Nezame no sode no	The scent of flowers in my sleeve
Hana no ka ni	Is what awakes me
Kaoru makura no	On a pillow richly fragrant
Haru no yo no yume.	With the brief spring night of dreams.

The effect is all the more ethereal because cherry blossoms lack in reality the fragrance attributed to them here. As the frost of the earlier poem conveys a symbolically frost-chilled experience, so here the fragrance symbolizes the world created. Such descriptive symbols, cast over with varying degrees of Komachi's passion and Teika's ethereal beauty, are major elements in the poetry of Princess Shokushi and Shunzei's Daughter.

Ariie, whose best poems sometimes seem to consist of an active verb or two with a balance of imagistic nouns, employs imagery in ways that resemble the use of symbols by the two women. In a winter poem, "Snow at the Village of Fushimi," that we have seen earlier in a sequence, snow is a symbol of frustrated love (*SKKS*, VI: 673).

Yume kayou	Beneath the piling snow
Michi sae taenu	The bamboos of Fushimi village
Kuretake no	Crack loudly in the night—
Fushimi no sato no	Even the path to love in dreams collapses
Yuki no shitaore.	Into waking from the sounding snow.

Ariie uses snow as a symbol of frustration both in real love meetings and in dream meetings. The last three lines consist of five nouns joined by the possessive particle *no,* an effect impossible in English, as is also the play on the word *Fushimi.* It means the place; it also means "lying down and seeing" and therefore is an "associated word" (*engo*) with "dreams" (*yume*); *fushi* also means "joint," and is an *engo* with "bamboos" (*-take*). Such a combination of complexity, romance, and symbolic passion typifies one of Ariie's styles at its best. But he also adapts from Shunzei the search for essences and sometimes weaves the result into a tight group of images, as in "The Spirit of Travel" (*SKKS*, X: 961). Something of its texture can perhaps be communicated by reducing the syntax as far as English will allow.

Fushiwabinu	I lay in suffering.
Shino no ozasa no	An instant's pillow of cuttings
Karimakura	From the small bamboos:
Hakana no tsuyu ya	The transience of dew and tears:
Hitoyo bakari ni.	The anguish of a single night.

The seminal ideals of Shunzei, the spiritual force of Saigyō, and the creative brilliance of Teika affected all the important poets of the age. A final poem by the Priest Jien (1155–?1225), who is sometimes dismissed as a rhetorician, is representative, for it shows how, to the poet, man's deprivation might also have a magical beauty. The poem (*Shūgyokushū* in *K. Taikei*, X, 740) is also appropriate because it echoes the beautiful anonymous poem on dawn at Akashi Bay with which the last chapter concluded.

Kajimakura
Nezame ni fukaki
Asaborake
Yume mo ato naki
Fune o shi zo omou.

Pillowed above the oars
And deep in sleep until dawn breaks,
I wake to find no ship:
The one that bears my longings in the
dream
Has borne me in the daylight from this
boat.

The fusion of past and present, dream and reality, beauty and suffering, object and mystery, confirms the genius of this age of Japanese poetry.

CHAPTER SEVEN

Major Poets from 1241 to 1500

Fifty years ago, accounts of the poetry written by the court ended with the eighth of the imperial collections, the *Shinkokinshū* (ca. 1206), or possibly with the ninth, the *Shinchokusenshū,* which was completed by Teika about 1234. The old view, which still muddles some historians' conceptions of the court, was that the *Shinkokinshū* was a late last flowering of a now powerless court society and that thereafter there was, so to speak, poetic silence until *nō* appeared in full growth in the fifteenth century, the linked form *renga* flowered in the fifteenth and sixteenth centuries, or *haikai* flourished under Bashō in the seventeenth century. We all like clearly defined beginnings and endings to our historical periods, but the fact is that the court retained great vitality if not great power until the anarchy of the fifteenth century, and, even until the death of the Renga Priest Sōgi in 1502, distinguished poetry was written in the court tradition. What actually happened, as recent Japanese scholarship has shown more and more clearly, is that all the political upheavals could not arrest the natural continuity and development of poetry. The continuity is in the tradition defined by Tsurayuki, although the development leads us by imperceptible steps from a poetry of the court to a poetry of the camp and temple. For poetry, the transition to "feudalism" did not require the brutal chaos of civil war.

Before the soldierly and monkish poets took over from the courtiers, the courtiers enjoyed a last period of creativity. If the late classical period (1241–1500) is not as brilliant as the early classical period or as profound as the mid-classical period, it is nonetheless memorable for the intensity it brings to poetry. Its historical importance is patent; at this time Japan was menaced by a Mongol invasion, divided by rival imperial lines, and threatened with chaos because of the possible collapse of the military government at Kamakura. For poetry it was a time of crisis too, though the story of the quarrels among Teika's descendants is at once amusing and depressing. They quarreled both over poetry and over the estates of his son Tameie (1198–1275) who, while young, had vacillated between poetry and court football (*kemari*).

Tameie's eldest son, Tameuji (1222–86), headed a branch of the family known as Nijō. Tameuji was master of family property and the poetic inheritance of the house until his father curtailed his inheritance by a new will granting some property to sons by a younger wife, a woman best known by her religious name, the Nun Abutsu (d. ca. 1283). She sought to get what had been willed her sons by appeal to the lawcourts at Kamakura, which she visited on a journey described in her *Diary of the Waning Moon* (*Isayoi Nikki*). Her son Tamesuke (b. 1263) eventually got his property and was progenitor of the Reizei line of the family. In poetic as well as family matters the Reizei line made cause against the dominant Nijō branch by joining with the middle branch, the Kyōgoku, descended from yet another son of Tameie's, Tamenori (1226–79). For our purposes it is enough to say that the senior Nijō line was very conservative in poetry, thinking that in these latter days it was better to stick with the tried and true; in contrast, the junior Kyōgoku-Reizei lines were highly experimental. It is as though the second half of the slogan of Shunzei and Teika —"old words, new heart"—was taken by the Nijō poets to be suitable for an earlier age of great innovators but inappropriate for their later generation, who would be well advised to use old words and old heart. The Kyōgoku-Reizei poets appeared to think quite the contrary, that old words were much less significant than new heart; they must have recalled that even Teika himself had manipulated the old words to speak of a waiting night and a darkening wind. Neither side took the poetic inheritance in the fashion left them, and their poetic differences were at once irreconcilable in themselves and embittered by struggles for family property and support of rival imperial lines.

The result of the struggles of various kinds was that the conservative Nijō line won most of the battles for prestige and political influence, but that the Kyōgoku-Reizei families triumphed in creating a valid poetic tradition. Of the last twelve of the twenty-one imperial anthologies, ten were compiled by Tameie, by the Nijō line descending from him, or by its allies. Only two (which in quality outbalanced the others) were compiled by the Kyōgoku-Reizei adherents. The former of these, the *Gyokuyōshū*, was compiled by a major poetic and political figure, Kyōgoku Tamekane (1254–1332), about 1313 or 1314. It contains 2,796 poems,* more than any other imperial collection, apparently because Tamekane feared that he and his friends might have no second chance to compile an imperial anthology. There was, however, to be another, the *Fūgashū*, completed about 1345. Emperor Hanazono (1297–1348), himself one of the best poets of his generation and one of the most appealing of Japanese emperors in his personality, took the unprecedented step of not bothering to commission anyone to compile the collection but of doing it himself. In addition to these two imperial anthologies there were numerous personal collections and the *Shin'yōshū*, compiled about 1381, which was intended as an imperial anthology. It was sponsored, however, by the junior imperial line of Emperor Go-Daigo after he had rebelled against the Kamakura authorities and had been forced by various rivals to set up court in Yoshino. The *Shin'yōshū* has some military touches that forecast things to come.

The Nijō line may be left in its own dusty conservatism, for if it produced many poems, it did not produce much poetry. The Kyōgoku-Reizei poets are another matter. In the war of words between the two factions, the innovating poets were forced to set down and justify their principles. Consideration of their ideas will assist in understanding why they wrote the kind of poetry they did and in understanding their poems. The modification of Shunzei and Teika's preference for traditional words can be seen in *Lord Tamekane's Poetic Notes*. Tamekane was the major critic and poet of the period, astute enough to begin by praising the *Man'yōshū* and to

---

* Since the emphasis of this and the two preceding chapters has been on individual short poems, it should be noted that poems were usually composed for integrated sequences, and that techniques of progression and association integrated them in imperial collections. The *Gyokuyōshū* is a poetic whole of 13,980 lines.

end by echoing Tsurayuki's Preface to the *Kokinshū,* as if to justify his approach.

> At the time of the *Man'yōshū,* poets gave direct expression to
> what they felt in their hearts, not hesitating to say the same thing
> twice ... making no distinction between poetic diction and ordi-
> nary speech, they simply followed the dictates of their heart and
> said things just as they wished.*

The doctrine of spontaneous creation is of course traditional, but
the call for a poetic language like ordinary speech is revolutionary,
too revolutionary in fact to have been feasible. What Tamakane
really meant was that the creative poets of his generation wanted
to show their newness of "heart" by experimenting with the
"words" or the materials of poetry. Occasionally, it is true, we
do get images we feel no other period would produce, as is shown
by one of Emperor Hanazono's poems (*FGS,* XVI: 1764).

Ato mo naki	No trace remains
Shizu ga iei no	Among all the crumbling hovels
Take no kaki	Of their bamboo fences,
Inu no koe nomi	And only a dog breaks the silence,
Okubukaku shite.	Barking from the hindmost shack.

Some Chinese poets and an occasional Japanese eccentric had written about dogs. But for an emperor to write a formal poem on
such a subject and with so little elegance of imagery is truly remarkable. The bending of language in ways like reversed diction
shows that the Kyōgoku-Reizei poets were seeking freedom to
force language in "poetic" as well as in "prosaic" directions. They
were following those of Teika's imitators whose tricks with language produced what certain scandalized contemporaries called
Darumauta, or Zen Poems, Nonsense Poems. But the new poets
were seeking not imitation so much as the creation of a new world
of poetry, and they found that they could not create with a new
"heart" unless they used new "words."

Their most fundamental decisions over words were those that
polarized tendencies dating back several centuries. For instance,

* Tamekane, *Tamekane Kyō Wakashō, NKGT,* IV, 110.

they made a distinction between seasonal and love poems. By no means always, but again and again the seasonal poems are entirely imagistic and the love poems entirely nonimagistic. This kind of change is most typical of the age in that it does not really involve a radical change (such as flooding poetic language with ordinary speech); and one would not need to look long before finding entirely imagistic seasonal poems in the preceding period or entirely nonimagistic love poems in the period before that. And yet there is a new quality in the results of such a decision, as two poems will show, the first an autumn poem (*FGS*, VII: 664) by Lady Eifuku Mon'in (fl. ca. 1310).*

Someyaranu	As it grows weaker,
Kozue no hikage	The setting sun among the branches
Utsurisamete	Does not tint the leaves;
Yaya karewataru	Under the trees the grasses on the hills
Yama no shitakusa.	Wither slightly in the dimming rays.

For a love poem we may take this (*FGS*, XIII: 1297) of Lady Junii Tameko (fl. ca. 1290).

Waga kokoro	O my heart,
Urami ni mukite	If you are turning to resentment,
Uramihate yo	Do so to the limit,
Aware ni nareba	For if you turn to weaker sorrow
Shinobigataki o.	It will be impossible to bear.

The common impulse behind two such different styles is suggested by Tamekane in his statement on seasonal poetry.

> In order to express the true nature of the natural scene, one must focus one's attention and concentrate deeply upon it.... Therefore, if you try to harmonize your feelings with the sight of cherry blossoms in spring or with the autumnal scene, and if you express them in words without allowing anything to intervene between your feelings and the scene, then your work will become one with the very spirit of heaven and earth.†

---

* Lady Eifuku Mon'in (Eifuku Mon'in Naishi) is not to be confused with Empress Eifuku (Eifuku Mon'in)—the Lady took her name from service with the Empress. Many of the women poets, like Tameie's descendants, have confusingly similar names.

† Tamekane, *Tamekane Kyō Wakashō*, NKGT, IV, 109.

If the other remark quoted from his *Poetic Notes* has asked for new "words," this asks for intense "heart." Absolute focus and a union with the experience treated are necessary—the influence of Zen Buddhism is plain here—so that it is at least logical that the seasonal poems in their intensity should consist of images alone, and the love poems in their intensity of subjective general language alone. That is hardly the only possible inference from Tamekane's remark, but it does give us an explanation for different styles and for new poetic aims.

The freedom Tamekane sought with "words" was a freedom for intense scrutiny of experience. One poem after another winds up emotions or images to the breaking point, and they sometimes go beyond to an unexpected metamorphosis. The symptom of such scrutiny is the focus upon a crucial moment, or a crucial directed action, or both. Such closely focused examination often reveals the beauty of the commonplace or the surprises of love's agony, and it is in such realms that the poets not only showed the new "heart" of their poetry but also the debt they owed to Sung poets and to Zen Buddhist priests. Perhaps they also revealed the uncertainty with which they faced the future, because neither their political party nor their poetic styles seemed to have much chance of survival. To find beauty in the commonplace and significance in a brief moment suggests an intensity that may have been bred by the fear that their work might never be known.

No poet of the age stands as high as Teika does among the giants of his age. There are, however, fifteen or twenty truly accomplished poets, of whom the most striking in personality and poetry are Tamekane and Empress Eifuku (1271–1342). Among the other major poets, two of the finest are Lady Jusammi Chikako (fl. ca. 1300) and Emperor Fushimi (1265–1317), whose personalities are less distinct than those of Tamekane and Empress Eifuku, but whose best poetry is not noticeably inferior. Tamekane shows the intensity he urged for seasonal poems in "On Spring Rain" (*GYS,* I: 83).

Ume no hana	The plum in flower
Kurenai niou	Suffuses with a crimson glow
Yūgure ni	The early dusk,
Yanagi nabikite	In which the willows bend to earth
Harusame zo furu.	And the spring rain softly falls.

But the technique of creating as much lovely detail as possible is not new. For the new both in aim and in method, we must consider his poem on a changing moment at dusk (*FGS,* VIII: 794).

Furiharuru	The running hail
Niwa no arare wa	Falls, then stops, and falls again
Katayorite	In patches on the garden;
Iro naru kumo zo	And the beautifully colored clouds
Sora ni kureyuku.	Grow dark in passage through the sky.

The sensibility of the speaker in such poems is an important bond between the poet—who is supposed to enter into contemplative union with the scene—and the reader. Such a poem, read in foreign dress (or for that matter, by some who have more Japanese than poetry in them) could be thought merely imagistic, merely descriptive of a lovely scene that does not much matter. But read carefully, with full attention to what the author expected, or what any author has a right to expect—respect for his art—it can be seen to imply much more. We "must focus" our "attention" on the natural scene of his poem; we must "concentrate deeply on it." And if we do, we will see that the poetry of a great political figure, experienced critic, man of the world, and religious person like Tamekane must not be dismissed easily.

The readiest way to approach the poem is through examination of its situation and imagery. The speaker is implied to be gazing from indoors or from a verandah outdoors into his garden. The intermittent hail falls here and there, crossing the garden. As in so many poems of the period, this section of the poem ends with the conjunctive and gerundive modal morphemes, *-ite,* so joining the first three lines in a subordinate conjunctive way to the last two. In the concluding two lines, the speaker has looked up to the sky, where he might expect to find the cause of such a strange phenomenon as that of the running, intermittent hail. Simply put, the hail comes from clouds that are moving across the sky at dusk. But the strangeness and energy of the hail below is founded on a beauty that dies, in clouds that go off, leaving the Void of a night sky. That is where the speaker and the reader are also left: our attention has been startled by sudden hail, our hearts have been pleased by colored beauty in gentle motion, and our spirits have been shown that all dissolves into darkness and empty sky. Unlike Saigyō and his contemporaries, however, Tamekane does not leave us chilled with full darkness symbolic of man's state. Tamekane's contemplation is such that it suggests if not, in a word, Zen Buddhism and its enlightenment, then at least a revelation: there is order to even the most apparently disordered nature, and the Phenomenal yields to the Void when enlightenment comes.*

The particular terms of the poems may of course vary considerably. Another poem describes such natural force as a gradual movement toward the speaker; or to regard it differently, we are led to follow the speaker's intense gaze (*FGS*, IV: 398).

Matsu o harau	Ruffling down the pines,
Kaze wa susono no	The wind at dusk tumbles upon the grasses
Kusa ni ochite	Of the foothill plains below;
Yūdatsu kumo ni	The rain vies with the racing summer clouds
Ame kiou nari.	To be the first to bring the evening shower.

The wind "tumbles" (*ochite*) rather than blows; and rain vies (*kiou*). Both are unusual diction for court poetry; both are new "words." Since the wind and the rain are approaching, the clouds and their rain seem to compete in the race toward the speaker. It is in the close scrutiny of such natural forces and the attempt to feel in tune with their energy that the emphasis of Tamekane lies, and in this is the new "heart." His purpose is not to seek out the depths of tonal resonance or to make nature symbolize man, as poets of the preceding period had. Nature and man now are seen as cooperating: observation provides an insight, and the intensity of scrutiny usually yields to an implied assurance.

Empress Eifuku, probably the most striking love poet of the period, shows the same intense scrutiny in dealing with her subject, as one of her best poems shows (*FGS*, XIV: 1355).

Itoioshimi	Though I alone am anxious
Ware nomi mi oba	And do not wish to hate myself so much
Ureuredo	That I lose hold of life,
Kou naru hate o	There is nobody who understands
Shiru hito mo nashi.	How far I suffer as I love.

* Sir Charles Eliot, *Japanese Buddhism* (London, 1959), is the most useful for students of court poetry.

Here, the force is within the speaker, and it is that force which requires the closest perception and apperception alike. Under the pressure of such close scrutiny, the experience she treats—and similar experience treated by other poets of the age as well—changes surprisingly (*GYS*, XII: 1707).

Yowarihatsuru	In my grieving heart,
Ima wa no kiwa no	Weakened now by your betrayal
Omoi ni wa	To the point of death,
Usa mo aware ni	Even misery takes on pathetic beauty
Naru ni zo arikeru.	And my bitterness is gone.

The transformation is entirely unexpected—by the speaker and ourselves. The same process of metamorphosis can be observed in more complex form in one of her most attractive seasonal poems (*FGS*, II: 189).

Hana no ue ni	The evening sun
Shibashi utsurou	Flickers upon the cherry blossoms
Yūzukuhi	With a moment's light,
Iru to mo nashi ni	And though it does not seem to set,
Kage kienikeri.	Its glowing melts away.

The moment described in the first three lines is extended by a kind of slow motion, and within that period a change takes place almost imperceptibly. The moment becomes a lengthened interval while, in contrary fashion, stasis is made change—precisely because the intent gaze of the dedicated observer can discover such elements where casual viewing would see only humdrum nature. The melting scene of this poem resembles the transformations of the love poems. What is new in this preoccupation of the age is partly the handling of the imagery: it is highly unusual to treat a setting sun as the central feature of a poem including cherry blossoms. But what is more fundamentally creative is the sense of the dynamism of nature and the human spirit, of an inner force that leads not only to change but also to frequent metamorphosis or enlightenment.

If Empress Eifuku showed that her seasonal poetry followed the emphases of her love poetry, another poem by Tamekane, now on love, reveals how far he too followed in devoted scrutiny that which transforms itself under the pressure of such close examination (*GYS*, XIII: 1768).

Tsuraki amari	So great my misery
Ushi to mo iwade	That I have passed my days reluctant
Sugosu hi o	To speak aloud of suffering,
Uraminu ni koso	Till now my exhaustion is complete
Omoihatenure.*	And my bitterness toward you disappears.

The dedicated "heart" of such poems is expressed in their very difficult words. A close paraphrase of the poem just given might run: "Painful too much / Not saying even misery / The days which pass / Resenting extremely / Have come certainly to end of feeling." Tamekane and Empress Eifuku wrote both seasonal and love poems, and they shared a scrutiny so intense that reality might change under their burning gaze. The organization of Tamekane's poems seems less mannered, and they are more given to consideration of outside forces; the poetry of Empress Eifuku is more rhetorical than Tamekane's and, as befits the preoccupations of an inheritor of Komachi, more given to passion within the self.

Lady Jusammi Chikako treats subjects like those of the other two with rather less force but with greater delicacy. In "A Moor in Late Autumn" (*GYS*, V: 819) she, like Tamekane, arranges the natural phenomena in a movement, this time away from the speaker.

Nobe tōki	The wind blows,
Obana ni kaze wa	Swelling in the pampas grasses
Fukimichite	Wide across the moors,
Samuki yūhi ni	And in the cold of the evening sun
Aki zo kureyuku.	Autumn darkens to its close.

The poem seems at first glance to celebrate the meagre and soul-piercing beauty loved by Saigyō. And in a breeze swelling in plants or in darkening autumn we seem to have Teika's language. But the focus is very clearly on a single natural event, and that occurring so much at a moment that the poem is founded on a metamorphosis from physical, spatial movement to temporal. Chikako

* Following the text in *Kokka Taikan* rather than that in *Kokka Taikei*.

excels in description, perhaps in accuracy of feeling. But Saigyō and Teika are more profound. One of her love poems, on "Love Promises Broken," takes the intense experience of love as far as it will go and then breaks down (*GYS*, XII: 1702).

Higoro yori	In recent days
Uki o mo ushi to	I can no longer say of wretchedness
E zo iwanu	That it is wretched,
Ge ni omowazu mo	For I feel my grief has made me
Naru ka to omoeba.	No longer truly capable of grief.

There is less feverishness, almost a calm, in such misery, and, although the language of the poem is extremely elliptical, the transformation—from wretchedness to a state beyond words and even beyond understanding—seems more natural than the changes in Empress Eifuku's poems.

Another, less distinguished, poem by Chikako will show the kind of influence Zen Buddhism was having when its effect was direct rather than absorbed as in the preceding poems. It is composed "On the Full Moon of the Eighth Month" (*GYS*, V: 684) and uses a traditional religious emblem, the moon, as its central image.

Onozukara	Long since clouded over,
Sumanu kokoro mo	This heart of mine has now cleared up
Sumarekeri	Of its own accord—
Tsuki wa narete zo	It is good to gaze continuously
Miru bekarikeru.	Until one has absorbed the moon.

Although the three chief concerns of Zen Buddhism—contemplation, enlightenment, and moral improvement—emerge in the allegory, the statement also tells us how closely the poets looked on their poetic world.

The best poetry of Emperor Fushimi (1265–1317) concerned seasonal and religious topics, but he shared the concerns of language, organization, and perception with the other poets. Tamekane had said that poets in the *Man'yōshū* had not hesitated to say the same thing twice. In a poem on autumn lightning Fushimi shows no compunction in using three related words for light, in addition to lightning itself (*FGS*, VI: 566).

Nioi shirami	So white the glow,
Tsuki no chikazuku	As the moon approaches closer
Yama no ha no	To the rim of hills,
Hikari ni yowaru	That its brightness greatly weakens
Inazuma no kage.	The flashes of the lightning there.

There is nothing very novel about treating the autumn moon, but to treat it not only at the time just before it rises above the hill but also at the moment when it absorbs the force of streaking lightning—that is new. Another poem by Fushimi on "The Wind" (*GYS*, XV: 2172) offers one of the many contemporary scenes of natural phenomena ordered into patterned movement.

Hibikikuru	The wind comes on,
Matsu no ure yori	Rumbling first among the pine trees,
Fukiochite	Blowing from their tops
Kusa ni koe yamu	And falling on the slopes below
Yama no shitakaze.	Till its voice grows silent in the grass.

To be seen as patterns, natural events must not only be observed but be observed carefully. Instead of natural description used symbolically for man, the new description implies a human focus of mind on the scene, until the observer becomes "one with the very spirit of heaven and earth." Apart from the religious implications for the time, one can see that in practice once nature and human scrutiny are brought together, nature inevitably takes on subjectivity—and the process of apprehension itself seems to take on a reciprocal objectivity. One or the other, or both, of the reciprocal processes may be emphasized in late classical poetry, but both are inherent in the practice as well as criticism of the age.

Such novelty in the very conception of poetry is the most creative feature of the age. There are others, not only in words but in themes—for example, the seasonal vagueness of Fushimi's poem just given. Like many in the period, it is classified under "miscellaneous" (*zō*), a classification that had long existed but that came to have greater significance to the Kyōgoku-Reizei poets—there are five long books of Miscellaneous Poems in the *Gyokuyōshū*. The classification implies that no one formal category, such as a season, predominates. The increased popularity of this heterogeneous category implies that poets were trying new themes with which they might free themselves from old conceptual frameworks.

Another development in the poetry of the age is the superior quality of its religious allegory. Its metaphorical procedure employs a closed parallelism using natural images to convey, however indirectly, religious significance, so, in a sense, combining in allegory the pure imagery of the seasonal poems with the generalization of the love poems. The only drawback to the religious poetry is the great difficulty we have in understanding it. Emperor Fushimi wrote "On the Topic, 'The Three Dogmas Are Not One Dogma, Nor Are They Three Dogmas'" (*FGS*, XVIII: 2057).

Mado no to ni	Better to hear
Shitataru ame o	The rain outside my window
Kiku nabe ni	Tapping as it drops,
Kabe ni somukeru	I turn my midnight lamp around,
Yowa no tomoshibi.	Dimming its light against the wall.

We are mystified and yet intrigued by such a poem. Its last two lines echo Po Chü-i, the ninth-century Chinese poet, and the three dogmas referred to in the title are the Void, the Phenomenal, and the Mean. Essentially, the separation of the senses shows that the dogmas are not one, but their association in the scene shows them not to be three. It is an attractive poem, in both its cadence and its treatment of a subject about as alien to poetry, as normally conceived, as the idea of the three cardinal virtues. The poem shows the great gentleness of Fushimi's poetry, a gentleness that retains the force of poetic scrutiny characteristic of the age but without the agitation of Empress Eifuku or Tamekane.

Yet even in so attractive, so benign a poem, the closed allegory does not conceal from us the fact that the fundamental concerns of the age are after all integral to the now lengthy tradition of court poetry. We have observed that throughout the centuries the crucial aesthetic problem was to define the role of the speaker or poet—that is, of man—in relation to a larger reality of which he is an uncertain part. And we have seen that such definition entailed complex human responses encompassing, and often combining, joyous affirmation and blank desolation. The late classical period clearly belongs to the ages of poetic faith in showing deep awareness of such paradoxes, both in its criticism and in its poetry. The active scrutiny of the poets yields the turns and surprises, the minute distinctions, and the many agitations of this poetry. It conveys a greater, or at least a more persistent, psychological awareness, and it owes a great deal to the self-induced understanding through intuition taught in the discipline of the Zen Buddhist priests. The activity of their poetry makes an Empress Eifuku or a Tamekane seem more robust than, say, a Princess Shokushi or a Narihira. It is also true, however, that the robustness and agitation sacrifice some fineness and depth. Something of the joy goes from the world when it is so actively and minutely scrutinized.

| Yaya karewataru | Under the trees the grasses on the hills |
| Yama no shitakusa. | Wither slightly in the dimming rays. |

The observation is very keen, but by that very token there is less of the open celebration of the world than we find in earlier periods. What we have is better detailed; but it is often less significant. Similarly, when one is so aware of one's own consciousness, it is less life's overwhelming darkness that claims attention than the smaller shadows cast by one's own psyche (*GYS*, XII: 1707).

Yowarihatsuru	In my grieving heart,
Ima wa no kiwa no	Weakened now by your betrayal
Omoi ni wa	To the point of death,
Usa mo aware ni	Even misery takes on pathetic beauty
Naru ni zo arikeru.	And my bitterness is gone.

This is true psychological reality, but Empress Eifuku does not, or does not seem to, discover the fuller reality of love expressed so well by Narihira and Komachi.

Before turning one's own lamp away from the Kyōgoku-Reizei poets, the better to hear them, a last poem by Fushimi will serve to remind us that they were also conscious of their connection with the courtly past. His "On the Spirit of Stopping Overnight on a Journey" makes the point perfectly (*GYS*, VIII: 1239).

Kajimakura	Pillowed above the oars—
Hitoyo naraburu	Will these ships now lying side by side
Tomobune mo	For a night's companionship
Asu no tomari ya	Anchor in loneliness for tomorrow's sleep,
Ono ga uraura.	Each in the harbor of its separate bay?

The poem is an allusive variation on that by the Priest Jien given at the end of the last chapter. As Fushimi knew, Jien's poem is itself an allusive variation on the anonymous *Kokinshū* poem on dawn at Akashi Bay. The resonance is very nice and shows that, for all their innovations, the Kyōgoku-Reizei poets were court writers in the mainstream of development.

The tradition continues, though in special terms, with the four important poets who take us in their poetry from the court to the "feudal" world of camp and temple and to such new forms as the linked verse, *renga*. The first, Imagawa Ryōshun, lived a very long life (1325–1420), and in it made a name for himself as a poet in the *waka** of the court tradition, as a *renga* poet, as an administrator, as a soldier, and as a critic. As a *renga* poet, he was most indebted to the influential Nijō Yoshimoto (1320–88), who played a major role in codifying the rules of *renga*. But in his *tanka* he was indebted to the innovating Reizei poets. An allegiance to Yoshimoto for *renga* was not necessarily a sign of conservatism, but adherence to the Reizei poets for *waka* was a sure sign of poetic liberalism. By the time he was twenty, he had had a moderately interesting poem included in the *Fūgashū* (XV: 1473), the second of the anthologies to be compiled by Kyōgoku-Reizei poets. The styles Ryōshun practiced emerge more distinctly, however, in his later work, as a few examples from his diary of a journey, *Travelings* (*Michiyukiburi*), will show. Interspersed in the fragmentary prose *continuo* are poems of many kinds, but frequently we see the full imagistic style of the Kyōgoku-Reizei poets, as in the following description (*Michiyukiburi, GSRJ,* XVIII, 566).

> Ōzaki no　　　　　At Ōzaki Point
> Ura fuku kaze no　　The breeze across the inlet hushes
> 　　Asanagi ni　　　　In the morning calm,
> Tashima o wataru　　And crossing above Tashima Island,
> Tsuru no morogoe.　The united voices of the cranes.

The use of images alone declares his poetic allegiance, as does his playing with the closely observed details of scenery—one action

---

* The term *waka* may be used to mean Japanese poetry in general, but throughout this chapter it refers to Japanese court poetry—*tanka, chōka, sedōka*—and does not include the later derivative forms such as *renga* and *haikai*.

stops so that another may begin. But the conception of the poem
is really timeless in its evocation of beauty, as can be understood
by a comparison with Kurohito's similar travel poem (*MYS*, III:
273; see p. 56 above) written some five centuries earlier.

Like the Kyōgoku-Reizei poets he admired, Ryōshun faced the
problem of maintaining a balance between experiment and tradition. And as with them, his most novel poems are not always the
most successful (*Michiyukiburi, GSRJ*, XVIII, 559).

Mononofu no	Because its warriors
Takeki na nareba	Have a name hard won for courage,
Azusayumi	Who would not bend
Yakage ni tare ka	Before the arrow village of Yakage,
Nabikazaru beki.	Strong as the soldier's birchen bow?

Here if anywhere, one might say, a new "heart" has entered poetry,
and indeed something of a soldier's experience in his early years
no doubt lies behind Ryōshun's conception. Yet the poem suffers
from having said everything at once, and perhaps from having had
not all that much to say. Admired as it sometimes is for its evocation of warriors' stalwart spirit, the poem is deficient in the depth
of meaning accumulated by generations of poets. Ryōshun is at his
best when he combines traditional and contemporary elements in
his poems, as yet another example from *Travelings* will show (*Michiyukiburi, GSRJ*, XVIII, 560).

Uchikawasu	Oh, to share the night
Tomone nariseba	In talking with these fisher-poets—
Kusamakura	For then the miseries
Tabi no umibe mo	Pressing the pillow-grass of travel
Nani ka ukaran.	Would no longer wash my seaside path.

The travel diary depicts the weary traveller, who would be willing
to stop his journey to spend the night with people who have proved
so surprisingly civilized as the fishermen of the area. But he must
go on, and, if he keeps going, so too will his sufferings continue.
Tabi no u- suggests the anguish of travel, and *umibe* evokes the
seashore. Similarly, *ukaran* plays on words suggesting floating and
suffering. Several earlier styles are combined into one, and perhaps
it is such skill that won Ryōshun his contemporary fame.

Ryōshun's position as a respected critic espousing Reizei ideals
led the Priest Shōtetsu (1381–1459) to send him poems for com-

ment, so beginning the succession of teacher-student relationships that was to provide the fifteenth century with its greatest poets. Shōtetsu is thought by some Japanese today to be the finest poet of the century; the twenty thousand poems of his personal collection, the *Sōkonshū,* show that he was also one of the most prolific poets of the whole court tradition. A hundred thousand lines of poetry may be thought remarkable in any lifetime. He was indeed an enthusiast, not only for the Kyōgoku-Reizei styles, but also for the earlier styles of Teika. As he said in his *Tale of Shōtetsu (Shōtetsu Monogatari*), which is one of the most significant pieces of Japanese criticism: "It would be difficult to find from ancient times love poems comparable to Teika's."* He admired *The Tale of Genji* as well, giving lectures on it and other works of early literary times.

Some of his best poems combine the intensity of older styles with a new religious repose. "Morning-Glories Next Door" suggests such calm in its tone and the beauty of court poetry in its sounds (*Shōtetsu Hyakushu* in *ZGSRJ,* XXVIII, 907).

Nakagaki no	No trace remains
Kage mo nokorazu	On the fence between the houses:
Shioruru ya	So they have withered!
Asahi suekosu	The morning sun has passed across
Asagao no hana.	The morning-glory's frail flowers.

Although he could not but have approved of the cadence, Ryōshun probably gave his verdict that the poem was the best of the hundred-poem sequence for another reason. Shōtetsu very skillfully handles the morning-glory emblem for worldly transience in a way seemingly as objective as the Kyōgoku-Reizei poets; yet he also evokes the human relevance expressed by the descriptive symbolism of the mid-classical poets. Another poem, "Parting Love," from the same sequence has less repose than intensity (*ZGSRJ,* XXVIII, 911).

Ukareyuku	As I take my leave,
Tama to dani miyo	Think of the dew along my path
Tsuyu harau	As my soul's tears
Mi wa shirotae no	Gemming the white sleeves covering us,
Sode no wakareji.	Sleeves parted by the light of dawn.

---

* Quoted by S. Hisamatsu, *Chūsei Wakashi* (Tokyo, 1961), p. 304.

Much of the best of both poems is present in yet another poem from the sequence, "Orange Trees in a Garden" (*ZGSRJ*, XXVIII, 906).

Tachibana no	Overgrown with moss,
Sakeru nokiba no	The eaves brighten with the blossoms
Kokegoromo	Of the orange trees;
Furuki itama ni	Through the old boards to my mossy robe
Sode no ka zo suru.	Comes the scent of sleeves of long ago.

Like Shunzei's Daughter before him, he has alluded to one of the magical anonymous poems of the *Kokinshū*.* The moss is that covering the dilapidated eaves of his priestly cell and is as well the color of his clerical garment. The scent is that of the perfumed sleeves of a woman the speaker had loved before becoming a priest. Shōtetsu seems all the more human a priest for conceiving of old attachments stirring memories in a tonsured head. In such poems he is original in both the limited sense of novelty and in the more fundamental sense of having created his own world, in which the magic of love reverberates through his own and his culture's past to harmonize with a priestly calm and assurance.

Shōtetsu's greatest student was the Bishop Shinkei (1406–75), who idealized such mid-classical poets as Teika and Shunzei and sought to bring to *renga* as well as to *waka* what he could revive of the ideals of "mystery and depth" (*yūgen*) and "ethereal beauty" (*yōembi*). The ideals came from court poetry, but in his own work the elliptical, glancing, packed style of *renga* gave the effect of Shōtetsu's intensity without its repose. His poetry is in fact more difficult even than Kamo no Chōmei's, which is saying a good deal. Since any attempt to express in English what his poems mean is certain to homogenize, as it were, his distinctive and pregnant obscurity, it may be useful to try to convey his meaning by rendering his words as explicitly as possible (*Shinkei Sōin Hyakushu* in *ZGSRJ*, XXVIII, 914).

---

* *KKS*, III: 139; given in Chapter V above, p. 99. The preceding poem is also an allusive variation, on one of Teika's finest love poems, *SKKS*, XV: 1336.

Sate mo mi ni	So then, for me
Munashiki kane no	is this the destination
Yuku sue ya	of the hollow bell's toll?
Tada nochi no yo no	Only an after world's
Yūgure no koe.	voice of dusk.

The elliptical style becomes a provocative challenge to our understanding. Now we may seek to be more interpretive.

> What comes to me
> Is the emptiness of the vesper bell
> Going—to what end?
> It is the voice of an evening
> That speaks but of the world to come.

It is not likely that even from such a rendering one would guess that the topic of the poem is "Love," or that the speaker is a woman whose lover no longer comes at the canonical lovers' hour of dusk. Now, the vesper bell is "empty," both because it brings no hope and because it symbolizes the emptiness of human existence in Buddhist thought. Whether such obliqueness intensifies poetic quality is no doubt a matter of taste. Most Japanese seem to prefer Shōtetsu's less packed style, but it can scarcely be doubted that in this and similar instances the technique of *renga* enriches older modes. We may consider another, yet more interpretive rendering.

> The fading bell
> Is indeed a presage of the emptiness
> Of life and hopes of love:
> Now the only voice I hear at evening
> Is this that speaks but of the world to come.

A second poem, from the autumn rather than the love section of his hundred-poem sequence, has a resonance recalling for us much that is finest in court poetry (*ZGSRJ,* XXVIII, 914).

Mushi no koe	The insects' voices,
Kaze no keshiki mo	And, across the grassy plain, as well
Kusa no hara	The wind's low tone—
Naki hito kou ka	Do they too speak of love for someone gone
Nobe no yūgure.	As twilight darkens over autumn moors?

The integration of dissimilar details may owe something to the poet's experience with *renga,* but though the autumn poem is less brilliant than that on love, its depth and naturalness seem to bear the weight of centuries of poetic experience.

The last of the four great fifteenth-century poets is the Priest Sōgi (1421–1502). If Ryōshun had come from a military family, Sōgi came as it were from no family at all, so humble were his origins. His rise to the priesthood as well as to the first position among *renga* poets of his day suggests the fluidity of Japanese society in the chaotic time between the court period with its nobility and the settled "feudal" period with its hierarchies. He studied *renga* under Shinkei but *waka* under the conservative Asukai Masayo (1390–1452), who adhered to Nijō principles and compiled the last imperial anthology, the *Shinshokukokinshū.* Like Shinkei, Sōgi was no doubt greater as a *renga* than as a *tanka* poet, but he was a major writer in both forms. He also shared the scholarly interests of Shōtetsu and managed to achieve a similar repose, as is shown in his "White Hydrangeas in the Evening" (*Sōgi Hōshi Shū,* in *GSRJ,* XV, 482).

Tsuki wa mada	Still the emergent moon
Yama no ha kuraki	Lingers dark behind the mountain rim,
Tasogare ni	But in the twilight
Hikari sakidatsu	Their radiance anticipates its light:
Niwa no u no hana.	The garden with white hydrangea flowers.

The quiet beauty may seem to have almost too much lassitude. To anyone thinking so, "Plum Blossoms Before the Moon" (*GSRJ,* XV, 480) gives an equally peaceful but more highly charged experience.

Yo o samumi	The night grown cold,
Ume ga ka chikaki	I pillow on my arm nearby the fragrance
Tamakura ni	Of the flowering plum,
Tsuki wa kasumite	As the spring breeze blows upon me
Harukaze zo fuku.	And hazy moonlight glistens in my tears.

The imagery and atmosphere that Teika or Princess Shokushi would have used for love has still its ethereal beauty, but now for a world of shaven priests.

Yet another poem, "The Bell of an Old Temple," shows Sōgi at his best, bringing together traditional elements with a force of personality at once new and harmonious with responses long proved in court poetry (*GSRJ*, XV, 489).

Yume sasou	Inviting dreams,
Kane wa fumoto ni	The sound of the mountain temple bell
Koe ochite	Tumbles on foothills,
Kumo ni yo fukaki	And with clouds the night grows deep
Mine no tomoshibi.	Where on a peak a lamp still glows.

Religious allegory comes naturally to mind: the light is a beacon of hope to one whom the bell invites to dreams of paradise amid the darkness of this world. Yet even as pure description the poem carries the attractive integrity of a priestly world made significant by the poetry of the courtly past.

Of these four poets of the fifteenth century, Shōtetsu and Ryōshun are probably rated highest for their *waka* by modern Japanese scholars. It goes without saying that we should attend to the judgments of people experiencing their own poetry. But to speak one's own preference: Sōgi seems to combine the qualities of the other three with a freshness and naturalness that are—whatever evaluation might be thought proper—remarkable at the end of a millennium of poetry. Of course in literary history all is continuity, and the only end is silence, and it is certainly true that these four poets exemplify the natural transition from *waka* to *renga* and thence to the linked *haikai* of Matsuo Bashō (1644-94) and others. All the same, Sōgi is a poet whose development follows naturally from late classical poetic ideals, and he may be regarded as the last great poet in the court tradition proper. Late classical poetry had begun in controversy and had gone on to explore a new intensity of poetic experience. It ended in a calm expressed by the rich voice of Sōgi. The achievement of Ryōshun and the three priests—Shōtetsu, Shinkei, and Sōgi—is remarkable by any standard and provides a fitting close to Japanese court poetry. It is fitting because its quality is worthy of what had gone before; the benediction is appropriately given by a priest.

Kumo ni yo fukaki	And with clouds the night grows deep
Mine no tomoshibi.	Where on a peak a lamp still glows.

CHAPTER EIGHT

Major Themes

The themes of Japanese court poetry are, of course, inherent in the meanings of individual poems or collections and in the concerns of a given age. Before proceeding to a discussion of major themes, however, it should be said that there lie, outside the scope of this discussion, other general matters of very great interest. Perhaps the most important of these in purely literary terms is the debt of Japanese poets to Chinese poetry, history, and art.* To a courtier like Tsurayuki, a knowledge of Chinese poetry was as much a part of his civilized equipment as a knowledge of Virgil was of Pope's. Other important matters, too, were familiar parts of the knowledge of courtiers—indigenous art, history, social order and function, politics, and customs. The importance of these and similar matters is evident, and adequate treatment of each would require a separate book at least as long as this; for us, it may be enough to typify one of them—the importance of China—by analogy. China gave court poets their classical heritage.

We must add to this by no means unfamiliar analogy some fundamental discriminations between the classical inheritance of a Teika and of a Milton. The first is that China was not a dead civilization. It was constantly undergoing indigenous development and was accessible, as ancient Greece and Rome never were, to a poet willing to journey by ship to get firsthand contact, or of course to those willing to get information second hand by talking to immigrants or returned priests. If we could talk with Homer or have latest news about Horace, we would undoubtedly find them now

---

* The great importance of the matter can be judged from the fact that since World War II the Japan Academy has given two of its annual prizes to books on the general subject.

harder to resist in outright imitation, and now irrelevant to poetry in our own language. Today our younger poets would be looking for ways to get to Rome to write like Catullus, and tomorrow they would wish nothing so much as to forget him and mind their own literary shop. In other words, they would respond essentially as the Japanese did to China, and we would then mean something very different when we spoke of "our classical heritage."

The second difference between these two classical heritages is that of language. The modern European languages are related and indebted to Greek and Latin, and therefore modern writers share with classical Greek and Roman writers certain fundamental assumptions about the potentialities of literary language. The Japanese, by contrast, never took over Chinese as a poetic language; they not only took the very radical step of excluding from their poetry Chinese words used in prose, but they also devised a Japanese phonetic syllabary that theoretically made Chinese characters unnecessary. More important, as many a courtier getting up his Chinese poetry must have found, Japanese and Chinese are completely different linguistic media: it is not just that Japanese is an agglutinative language and Chinese a synthetic one; it is that their syntactic, phonological, morphological, and semantic structures are wholly different. No adequate Western comparison is possible for the Japanese adaptation and radical modification of the Chinese written system to the very different language which is Japanese. But the difference between the two languages may be typified by the exclusion from court poetry of Chinese loan-words—as if an alien language written in runes borrowed words and alphabet from Rome but yet insisted upon retaining pure "runic" for poetry and altered the Roman alphabet so that it could not be read by Romans. In such a fashion, Japanese poetry was "protected" from its classical heritage, just as modern European literatures have been protected from theirs by virtue of the fact that classical Greek and Latin are "dead" languages.

In any contrast or comparison between the poetry of one civilization and that of another there is the danger of assuming extreme similarities or differences. Such contrasts or parallels are too radical to be of use. It is more relevant to examine the reasons for the emergence of certain themes in Japanese court poetry, keeping in mind that these themes—nature, man's place in the world, and time—are of central importance in any developed literature. We must try to get at them in ways particularly relevant to court poetry, because the question is one of form and feeling as much as of idea and scheme. The characteristic evidence is to be found in the imperial anthologies, and with them the sequences, poetry matches, and private collections derivative from them. It will be necessary to subsume the *Man'yōshū* with its lack of consistent form under the imperial collections.

The most striking thing about the theme of nature in Japanese poetry is its seeming ubiquity. If a few poems show no sign of it, love and religious allegories are based on it. Over and over again, indeed spontaneously, Japanese poets turned to nature as a means of expressing what is most fundamentally human; by it they represented life. Such a preponderance of interest in nature to the exclusion of some matters of great moment to Western poets can scarcely be doubted. But what is of even greater contrastive significance is that in Japanese poetry nature is also treated, so to speak, for itself. What is common in early Japanese poetry does not come into English literature until the eighteenth century. Earlier our doctrine of correspondence between nature and man prevailed, giving us a king of the beasts or a royal oak, but our fear of natural elements, believed to be in decay since the Fall of Man, did not allow in English poetry the loving treatment of natural life found in Japanese court poetry. It is appropriate that it was a Tsurayuki rather than a Dr. Johnson who used a natural metaphor in his fundamental statement about poetry—it takes root in the human heart and flourishes in the countless leaves of words, he said— or that he praises the frog singing in his fresh waters. Nature is to him real, beautiful, and good.

The question is, of course, why? And the obvious answer is that both of the principal Japanese religions, Shinto and Buddhism, contributed in their ways to a loving appreciation, and hence a celebration, of nature. Shinto gave Japanese poets two distinctive conceptions of nature: a belief in its purity and a sense of its vitality. Nature was closely involved in the ritual purifications and liturgy of the religion. The Great Shrine of Ise is astonishingly simple, even primitive, as a major center of religious worship, but the natural purity of the place is refreshing to any visitor, and surely there is significance in the fact that it is one of the very few public places that Japanese do not litter with twentieth-century debris. There is no question that Japanese inhabit a beautiful archipelago, but all the same the islands have acute extremes of temperature, earthquakes, and typhoons, all of which might have led to a religion of threat, guilt, and expiation. Instead, the greatest concern was with taboos, defilements, and purifications, associated with occurrences usually thought to be disorders of nature by early peoples—childbirth, menstruation, death. The important thing is that nature—water, wind, or the sacred *sakaki* tree—helped maintain or regain purity. Man had to avoid defilements: significantly, his chances were best within rather than outside nature. Without being explicitly philosophical about anything—without for example arguing for a natural monism—Shinto assumed a harmonious relation and a joyful response of man to his environment. It enabled Japanese, one might say, to be happy without telling them why, which may indeed be the only way to be happy for long. It will be remembered that Akahito's poem on the Yoshino Palace describes it as a Shinto shrine—praising the human in terms of the religious and natural (*MYS*, VI: 925; see above, pp. 68–69). Nature tinged with Shintoism is what lends beauty and purity to man's palaces and his life.

Nubatama no	The jet-black night
Yo no fukeyukeba	Deepens to a hush among the birches
Hisaki ouru	In the stream's pure bed,
Kiyoki kawara ni	Where the plovers raise their call
Chidori shiba naku.	Above the murmur of the stream.

Even at a later date, when one could look back from the splendid capital of Heiankyō (at what is now called Kyoto) to the former glories of Nara, many of which were Buddhist and not Shinto at all, it is the purity of natural beauty that symbolizes what is precious (*KKS*, II: 90).*

* The poem (*KKS*, II: 90) is attributed to the "Nara Emperor," Heizei (r. 806–9), which gives it a certain nostalgia; in fact, it is possible that the poem is one of the anonymous lyrics of the *Kokinshū*.

Furusato to	Even in Nara,
Narinishi Nara no	The capital that has become
Miyako ni mo	Our abandoned home,
Iro wa kawarazu	The cherry trees have blossomed out,
Hana wa sakikeri.	Unchanged in color from the past.

It is the English Victorians to whom we attribute the phrase "cleanliness is next to godliness," but to Japanese, cleanliness or purity was an aspect of spiritual life.

Shinto also gave to Japanese a conception of the animistic vitality or "divinity" of nature. Places had their geniuses, forces their individualities, the dead their vitality, and the spirits their presences. All the natural world was flourishing with life. That again is a belief common to many peoples, but what is particularly striking about Japanese animism is its benignity. The national mythology as recorded in the *Kojiki* and *Nihongi* often succeeds in being at once distressing and amusing, but in spite of its absurdities and its occasional repulsiveness, it does not interfere with nature. As Tsurayuki put it (*KKS*, V: 262):

Chihayaburu	Mighty they are,
Kami no igaki ni	The gods within this sacred shrine—
Hau kuzu mo	Yet even the vines
Aki ni wa aezu	Creeping in their precincts could not hold
Utsuroinikeri.	Against the autumn's tingeing of their leaves.

Hitomaro was equally emphatic in the overture to his Samine poem (*MYS*, II: 220).

Tamamo yoshi	O the precious land of Sanuki,
Sanuki no kuni wa	Resting where the seaweed glows like gems!
Kunikara ka	Perhaps for its precious nature
Miredo mo akanu	I never tire in my gazing on it,
Kamukara ka	Perhaps for its holy name
Kokoda tōtoki	It is the most divine of sights.
Ametsuchi	It will flourish and endure
Hitsuki to tomo ni	Together with the heavens and earth,
Tariyukan	With the shining sun and moon,
Kami no miomo to	For through successive ages it has come down
Tsugite kuru.	That the landface is the face of a god.

The place is divine; the land itself is a divinity. Here is one reason for the prominence of place-names in Japanese poetry—each has a local vitality, a life specially attractive and its own. Nor is the appeal of such ideas restricted to the early period. Even the Buddhist Priest Saigyō could write (*SZS*, XX: 1275) of his native religion in the inevitable imagery of nature.

Fukaku irite	Already deeply entered,
Kamiji no oku o	As I inquire of the pathway of the gods
Tazunureba	About what lies beyond,
Mata ue mo naki	Above me looms a matchless peak
Mine no matsukaze.	Where the wind sings in the pines.*

Such motives and assumptions were most obvious in the books of seasonal poems (traditionally, six of the usual twenty of an imperial collection) thought to be so important that they began the collection. As we have seen, their very arrangement is carefully considered. The first poem or more dealt with the coming of the new year, which was associated with the advent of spring in the old calendar, and the last poems of the sixth book (the normal pattern was two books for spring and two for autumn, one each for summer and winter) dealt with the end of the year. In between, the sequence of poems followed the seasons as they were observed, as they fitted in with the calendar of activities at court, and as they became conventionally organized in detail. Such a convention can be found among the spring poems, whose dominant image is the haze associated with the season. Other images such as the melting snow, the blossoming plum, the singing warbler, or the blooming and falling cherry blossoms are lovingly introduced and regretfully let go. The absence of arrangement by author or by chronology of composition allows for the chronology of nature. Nature is more important than giving a poet his due by collecting all his poems in one place at one time.

To many observers, the harmony between Buddhism and Shinto has been remarkable, and to some offensive. One ought not believe in Christ and Pan at the same time. As *The Tosa Diary* and other works show, the gods and the Buddha are invoked together for protection, and some of the imperial collections have Buddhist

* The poem is given as an example of Saigyō's attachment to Shinto by S. Hisamatsu, *Chūsei Wakashi* (Tokyo, 1961), p. 42.

and Shinto poems in adjoining books. When we observe a devout priest like Saigyō showing devotion to his native religion, one may evaluate the lack of dogmatism differently, but there is no question that the Japanese sought harmony rather than conflict between the two religions. Insofar as the harmony was real rather than merely formal, the Buddhist reverence for all sentient life could be held, with no sense of contradiction, with animistically inspired affection for nature, and poetry could make its business the exploration of the similarities. *The Tosa Diary* and *The Tale of Genji* showed in prose that Japanese could be frightened by perilous seas or typhoons, but it does seem significant that neither the almost fifty poems of the one nor the nearly eight hundred of the other touched on such fears. The element of celebration in Japanese poetry is most exalted and purest in the seasonal poems, and it is almost inevitable that the so-called lofty style (*taketakaki yō*) distinguished by court critics should have been devised not for epic struggle or tragic conflict but for description of nature. In their poetry, Japanese have looked upon nature without uneasiness and have loved it without remorse. It has always been a home, a source of repose and strength, to which they could return.

Nature may not of course be considered, as a theme, wholly distinct. We must recognize not only that man is involved with nature, but also that he introduces numerous complexities. Cotton Mather, the American Puritan, put it one way when he said that nature is the map and shadow (that is, reflection) of the spiritual estate of the souls of men. The Japanese soul found it possible both to love nature and to hunt; and Japanese have regarded death as a pollution, as well as a source of human sorrow. More than this, Buddhism brought with its rich philosophy and complex liturgy a weight of moral law, directed at man, so heavy that it might overburden his heart. Man was after all not to allow himself to be attached to the illusions of this world, and if even a mother's love for her child was thought by the austere to be an obstacle to salvation, what was to be said for the unsettled heart of Tomonori and others when they saw cherry blossoms fall? It was, we must understand, not nature that was cursed by a fall in some distant paradise, but the heart of man himself that created the problem, as a poem by Narihira, "On Cherry Blossoms at Nagisa Palace," makes clear (*KKS*, I: 53).

Yo no naka ni	If in this world
Taete sakura no	There ever was a time when cherry trees
Nakariseba	Failed in the blossoming,
Haru no kokoro wa	Then the responsive hearts of men
Nodokekaramashi.	Might answer to a tranquil spring.

The difficulty arose because man needed to seek the right and yet was bound to the wheel of karma, struggling with existence in this life to rise above the faults of previous existences, seeking to free the self from bondage to its world and itself so that it might become one with a universal being. But not only that; there were also in man forces for evil of which he had no knowledge, over which he seemed to have no control. In *The Tale of Genji,* the jealous Lady Rokujō has her spirit leave her body to torment her rivals for Prince Genji's favor, even to the point of her becoming a homicidal force. She only slowly comes to glimpse the full tragic nature of the force within her.

And yet, and yet—parents will love their children, men and women fall in love, and life is dear. Buddhism could be put aside as easily as Christianity, or its happier sides might be what men chose to look upon. At all events, Japanese poets chose to write of love, probably the most universal and deepest experience available to men and women of whatever rank. Love became the second great subject of court poetry, and in the imperial collections, poems about it were given the second prominent place, as the leading group in the second half of the collection. In detail, convention, and treatment, the love is a courtly love that was no more the possession of non-noble classes than was the *amour courtois* of the European Middle Ages, although both the Japanese and the European courtly versions have had profound effects on subsequent conventions of love in their cultures. What the dominant treatment of love in the anthologies implies is that it was considered to be the most essential or typical experience of one's private life. If love is "the subject of the comic Muse," it is for Japanese the very sad and beautiful *comédie humaine.*

Although the pattern of courtly love usually ended with the man's indifference and the woman's solitary anguish, we know from Japanese history and our own common sense that women may also have betrayed men or that love may have been happy and true. A number of Japanese romances do in fact have happy

MAJOR THEMES

endings and famously promising forever-afters. But as with nature, so with love: the poets developed a major theme character-
izing man's experience of life, and in treating love they showed—
especially in the misery endured by the woman—the loneliness,
the frustration, and the desolation of heart that man knows in this
world. The sorrow of love is the sorrow of life, the sorrow and the
beauty of man's relation to his fellows. One can see the development of the theme as successive generations devise their particular
treatments of love in their sequences and anthologies. The course
of love comes to have less and less happiness, more and more fore-
boding, and ever greater suffering. Like not a little else in life, its
joy is brief and its sorrow long. Even poets as early as Okura were
concerned about the matter; after speaking of the way the girls'
eager hands welcome those of their lovers, he insists that "youth
knows few such nights."

In order to understand for themselves and to express to others
the essential truth of love, both Japanese and European poets of
courtly love used profound images to sum up what all men might
be thought to feel. In the West there rose the identification of love
with death, which is treated in versions as different as *Tristan and
Iseult, Antony and Cleopatra,* and Freud's association of Eros and
Thanatos. In Japan, love was associated with dream; the Buddhist implication is clear. At its simplest, or most explicit, we get
the bewilderment of the Ise Shrine Priestess after her night with
Narihira, asking, "Was our night a dream? Reality? / Was I sleep-
ing? Or was I awake?" Far more profoundly we get Narihira's
reply, with its concluding challenge: "You who know the world
of love, decide: / Is my love reality or dream?" But the challenge
acknowledges his own wandering in "the darkness of the heart,"
an attachment to a human being which is as ill-advised as it is
natural. How uncertain man's understanding of himself is! The
rapture of Narihira's night has yielded all too quickly to a fading
but poignant memory in which the consciousness of folly has
turned a beautiful dream into a religious nightmare. Later poets
heighten the illusory quality of love by making the dream a dream
one sees on a spring night, which was proverbially brief, or by
making the sleep no more than a short dozing. One scarcely grasps
the dream before it is over, and the phrase "an unfinished dream"

(*mihatenu yume*) becomes more and more frequent with poets. So charged is this motif of dream that when the *renga* poets codified into their rules the implicit practice of the court poets, they decided that "dream" might be used only once in a hundred stanzas.

What gave such strength to the image is the Buddhist conception of the transience of experience, the lack of stay (*hakanasa*) in human affairs. Of course such transience was thought to underlie all worldly existence, but the poets grounded much of their understanding of it in their treatment of love. Yet in the Japanese conception, this anguished, transitory, dreamlike experience is particularly precious and attractive. The beauty, the illusion, and the anguish are to be prized, just as are the fear and pity of Aristotle's conception of tragedy, because to their poetic expression we owe much that illuminates and gives value to our otherwise inchoate lives. Understanding this, we are able to see how the same anguish could enter into, and harmonize with, the theme of nature in the seasonal poems of a collection like the *Shinkokinshū,* leading Saigyō to his admission (IV: 362):

Kokoro naki	While denying his heart,
Mi ni mo aware wa	Even a priest cannot but know
Shirarekeri	The depths of a sad beauty:
Shigi tatsu sawa no	From the marsh a longbill
Aki no yūgure.	Flies off in the autumn dusk.

And only understanding this are we able to see how Narihira could treat an experience of love in these terms (*KKS*, XV: 747).

Tsuki ya aranu	This is not that moon
Haru ya mukashi no	And it cannot be this is the spring
Haru naranu	Such as the spring I knew;
Waga mi hitotsu wa	I am myself the single thing
Moto no mi ni shite.	Remaining as it ever was.

It was by introducing man to nature that the poets brought human shadows on the bright beauty they loved, and by turning to nature they found relief from the agonies of their lives. What was most important for Japanese poets was that the two responses—the celebration and the sense of desolation—became intermingled, or rather realized themselves in each other, as moments of beauty in Mozart wring the heart with suffering pleasure.

It was consciousness of time, for nature and man alike, that was the basis of such mingled responses. The sense of transience was founded on Buddhist conceptions, and yet even in Buddhism there are such ordered concepts of time as the cause and effect relation between past and present that is implicit in karma. One of the commonest of all bases for ordering time is the progress of the seasons, and Japanese poets went out of their way to make another in the temporal progression of courtly love. When one considers such orderly progressions, devised in the face of transience or the mind-staggering eons of Buddhist providential history, one can see that the theme of time is one of the most complex in Japanese poetry and thought. (It is remarkable that the overtures of Hitomaro and Yakamochi, which deal so frequently with the national or personal past impinging on the present, appear to have no precedent in Chinese poetry, whose dominant historical concerns are cyclical and political. Why Japanese should have reacted in this way is no doubt due to deep national motives; whatever the reason, there is abundant evidence in court poetry to show the fact.) Indeed, it could be argued that there is no other theme that touches Japanese literature more deeply than time, and that its implications govern crucial Japanese conceptions of literary form.

Hitomaro's poem on discovering a dead man at Samine may be recalled as an example in which time is a dominant theme. (See pp. 48–49 above.) It begins with a statement of the timeless beauty and divinity of Sanuki Province, and the historical inheritance of generations of Japanese. Then it tells of the narrator's immediate past, bringing him to the dramatic present of his discovery of the dead man, and to a hypothetical present involving the dead man's wife. The treatment of time and timelessness suggests an ultimately benign world that yet admits human tragedy.

The treatment of time in the Samine poem is not very different from some by Western writers. For fundamental differences we must turn to later poetry. The tendency toward fragmentation in Japanese literature, leading to shorter and shorter poems, inevitably meant that the time span that could be meaningfully developed—whatever contrasts may have been insisted on in a given poem—became smaller and smaller. The emergence of successively briefer forms was a factor that necessarily led poets to emphasize moments in a transient flow or causal sequence. A longer English poem could build high walls against the flow of outer time; a shorter Japanese poem gave mute testimony to the stream. The shifting mutability, the sense of man's being involved in a ceaseless flow of time, is a major feature of Japanese poetry. The poets show full consciousness of that force, for if not all poets of all periods sought like the late classical poets to capture intense moments, they knew with Narihira that they were caught up in a scheme of temporal motion in which what seemed stable and what seemed to change testified all the more strongly to change. Who could be sure of what was real, of what was true?

It is significant that one of the most enduring forms of Japanese literature was the diary, and Japanese motives for keeping journals differed in emphasis from Western. Western motives are essentially memorial, to create a sense of the flow of time so that what has happened may be set down as it has happened. The stream of our consciousness—around mountainous events—is what interests us. The Japanese sought in their diaries to celebrate island-like moments of rich significance that might arrest, however briefly, the inexorable flow of time. Much of court fiction followed the example of Tsurayuki's *Tosa Diary* (ca. 935) in taking its aesthetic character from the poems it included. In poetic diaries, as in the contexts given to poems in other mixed genres, the attempt was to place the exalted moment in its context. Japanese of all periods have been interested in the contexts of poems, assuming a connection between a poem and the stream of the poet's own time that is astonishing to those of us brought up in fear and trembling of the autobiographical heresy. Over and over, Japanese wish to know what the context, what the larger temporal setting, of a poem may be. Or conversely, in such a very long story as *The Tale of Genji* the many, many poems celebrate the nature of the experience by capturing its essential character, by showing its wondrous worth amid the fluidity.

Such an excursion into the diary and the tale should remind us that the brief forms of single poems are not to be regarded as autonomous entities in the same sense as Western ones. Where those insist upon their liberty and separateness, Japanese poems proclaim their connectedness, their adhesiveness to situations, to a prose *continuo,* or to each other. Just as there is no question that the poetic forms are in themselves short, so is it certain that they form larger wholes for which there are very few Western analogies. We tend to think of units either in terms of highly subordinate stanzas, which could not possibly exist independently, or in terms of wholly independent formal wholes. It is precisely the area between that is occupied by the shorter Japanese forms, which are units but not mere parts, and full expressions but yet integers in larger units.

With Japanese conceptions of endless time spans articulated by religious cause and effect or inheritance from the past, it was natural that poets should seek workable wholes. Once again, the imperial collections provide the best guide for discussion. The absence of organization by author or chronology suggests both an emphasis on the poem as moment and the poem as an integrated part in a larger artistic and temporal whole. The three longest groups were of course the seasonal, the love, and the miscellaneous poems. (The books of miscellaneous poems were themselves commonly microcosms of the whole anthology form.) Two of the three at least were, then, integrated very obviously with a temporal scheme of progression that requires no Buddhism to understand. Once the potentiality of temporal progression was glimpsed, as it was in the first imperial anthology, other more complex techniques followed, bringing imagistic spatial progression and minute associations of imagery, diction, and rhetorical devices. The *Shinkokinshū,* which is in most ways the masterwork of integration by means of association and progression, even goes so far as to order its travel poems into a miniature history of Japanese poetry. (Some other groups were similarly ordered.) Only when the technique of association and progression had been developed to a great height did simple chronology occur to compilers as an added grace.

There are numerous complex interplays of time in the literary practices of the court. One person might read a romance aloud, while others who followed the narrative flow gazed upon illustrations of the section being read. Although the illustrations often had a kind of graphic movement of their own, they were an inevitably static accompaniment to narrative. Contrary mingling of forms was also common: poets would compose verses celebrating scenes on a screen, introducing such temporal concerns as the passing of spring, nostalgia for one's village, or contrast of past and present. For this, the art provided the fixed frame and the poetry the temporal *obligato*. The sequences, which we considered in their hundred-poem form in an earlier chapter, were themselves sometimes applied to poetry matches, giving as it were the unity of performance to a number of sequences composed by different poets. (Even poetry matches might be absorbed into the protean diary genre.) Methods of progression and association themselves had many variations. Usually the associative techniques led to clear connections between poems. But occasionally from the *Shinkokinshū* on, and strongly in the *Gyokuyōshū* and *Fūgashū,* less obvious relations were established between poems. It was common in the late classical period for the compiler of an imperial collection to put side by side two poems with no apparent association. Only by recognizing that together they created an allusive variation on an earlier poem that neither creator had intended could one see the connection.

It was not far from this technique of "distantly related verse" (*soku*), as it came to be called, in the anthology or the hundred-poem sequence to the linked-verse form, *renga. Renga* used a total of one hundred of the stanza halves of a *tanka*—five-seven-five stanza halves alternating with seven-seven halves—in such a way that any two halves made a poem. The relations between one unit and the next were sometimes very distant indeed, although rules of composition became extremely elaborate, partly to give form to what was otherwise unlikely to possess it, and partly to codify principles implicitly obeyed by the court poets. *Renga* sequences were composed by court poets in the mid-classical period, but mostly as a relief from the rigors of writing their *tanka* poetry and sequences. The new form was taken with increasing seriousness, however, so that in the late classical period it flourished alongside the older court forms. From *renga* it was even less far to *haikai*, originally a less serious linked form than *renga,* but in the hands of masters like Matsuo Bashō a very serious form indeed. The great alteration was clearly that from *tanka* sequences to *renga*; once that was made, post-court poetry was out of the egg.

But it emerged at a time, the mid-classical period, when in the opinion of many, the finest court poetry was being written. The continuity of development is not unlike the smooth temporal flow with sudden brilliant effects that one discovers in reading the court poems in their proper sequences.

What the various methods of integration and absorption imply is that the seemingly lyric moments of Japanese poetry are in reality temporal units attempting to arrest the endless flow of time in the sequences. If we have been slow to recognize such methods of integration and the temporal significance they carry, it is of course because Japanese themselves have recovered knowledge of the phenomena only recently. Unfortunately, only one full sequence has been translated to date.* As a result, the only adequate means of appreciating this major feature of Japanese poetry is to read the imperial collections or the sequences in the original. It remains true, as so often with all literatures, that certain major pleasures or realities remain largely hidden behind the wall of language.

Both the brief form of the *tanka* and the longer integrated form of sequence or anthology are results, then, of attitudes toward time. They speak eloquently of the precious moment that Tsurayuki declared for once and for all to be what Japanese poetry aspired to celebrate. They speak as well of the larger spans of time in the cycle of the seasons, in the story of human love, or in other patterns of human experience. Nature and man alike are subject to time, and although the valued moment may rise above time or may even intersect time and eternity, it is time that is at once man's ally and mortal enemy. It offers man the delights of the changing season and reminds him that love means betrayal, that life implies death.

---

* It is a sequence Teika put together from poems by other poets: see Brower and Miner, *Fujiwara Teika's Superior Poems of Our Time* (Stanford, 1967), which discusses the integration of the eighty-three poems. A famous *renga* has been translated into English (the *Minase Sangin Hyakuin,* Tokyo, 1956, translated by Kenneth Yasuda); for a sample of a *haikai* see Howard Hibbett, "The Japanese Comic Linked Verse Tradition," *Harvard Journal of Asiatic Studies,* XXIII (1960–61), 76–92. Isolated verses by Bashō, Buson, and others have, of course, often been rendered. The mixed genres of diary, tale, and travel record have often been translated; however, none of these gives the feeling of a poetic *continuum* that one gets by reading through an imperial anthology.

It is the moment, it is forever, and it is the continuity between—or permutations and combinations of all three. The re-examination of the poems we have considered would show at once how conscious their poets were of time, and how they embodied it into the situations, development, and themes of their poems.

Since time is so basic to reality and existence, its treatment in any poetry is of great significance. What is unusual about Japanese poetry is that its very forms not only bespeak a concern with time as a theme but also give an expression of it in the terms in which the poets believed time to affect human lives, in the small and in the large. In the literary functioning of time we are able to discover that music which harmonizes the joy of celebration and the anguish of desolation, responses so fundamental to court poetry. And it is also time that gives to such major poetic subjects as nature and man that continuity and energy which we take for life. Music and life are what Tsurayuki believed to be the peculiar possession of poetry; certainly he saw them in his own poetic tradition. Possessing these, it has a humanity that not even its difficult language can hide from foreign eyes or prevent from taking root in our hearts as well as those of Japanese.

Glossary

AWARE: Or *mono no aware* (literally, the suffering in things). The term suggests an anguish that takes on beauty or a sensitivity to the finest—the saddest—beauties. Both the condition and the appreciative sensibility are implied.

CHŌKA: "Long poem" of alternating 5 and 7 syllable lines, ending with an extra 7 syllable line. Often followed by one or more envoys in *tanka* form. Flourished in the first half of the eighth century.

CHOKUSENSHŪ: Imperial anthologies. The first three are often called *sandaishū* (collections of three eras), the first eight *hachidaishū* (collections of eight eras), and all twenty-one *nijūichidaishū* (collections of twenty-one eras).

DAI: The topic of a poem. As *dai* came to be set to make judgment possible in poetry matches, they became more conventional and complex.

DARUMAUTA: "Zen" or nonsense poems, a term of contempt used in the twelfth and thirteenth centuries for what were thought abuses of language or obscure conceits.

EN: Charm. Also used to designate a style of rich or captivating beauty. See *yōembi*.

ENGO: Word association. Relation of disparate elements in a poem by the use of a word that has or creates an "association" with a preceding word or situation, often bringing out an additional dimension of meaning and giving two expressions a secondary richness.

FŪRYŪ: Courtly elegance modeled on an essentially Chinese and Taoist concept (*fêng-liu*). See *miyabi*.

HAIKAI: (1) A form of *renga*, admitting humor or such unconventionalities as Chinese loan-words. (2) A form of serious linked verse practiced after the court period. (3) Discrete beginning stanzas (*hokku*) in *haiku* form.

HAIKU: (From *haikai no ku.*) The seventeen syllable poem of three lines of 5, 7, 5 syllables fixed as a discrete form after the Meiji Restoration (1868).

HAKANASA: Transience, lack of stay. (Adjective, *hakanaki.*) Buddhist conception of the temporal flux of worldly phenomena.

HON'I: Essential nature. Applied to the tone and treatment in poetry considered most effective in conveying the essential significance of an image or experience.

HONKADORI: Allusive variation. Recalling some words, basic situation, or conception of an earlier well-known poem (or other work) in a new poem, creating a new meaning that transformed the old in the new.

HYAKUSHUUTA: A sequence of one hundred *tanka*; other numbers were also common. The sequences were often modelled on parts, or the whole, of imperial anthologies.

IMPERIAL ANTHOLOGIES: See *chokusenshū.*

JIKAAWASE: A poetry match with oneself. A variation, developed in the twelfth century, of the *utaawase.* The poet would select topics, compose one or two rounds of poems on each, pit them against each other, and usually send them for judging to someone he respected.

JUKKAI: A topic (*dai*) introduced into collections in the twelfth century expressing personal grievance about the speaker's low state or failure to advance in the world.

KAKEKOTOBA: Pivot-word. Scheme of word play in which a series of sounds is used to mean two things at once by different parsings.

KARMA: See *sukuse.*

KASHŪ: (1) The poetic collection of an individual writer. (2) A work such as a diary (*nikki*) or tale (*monogatari*) sharing characteristics of a collection.

KOKORO: Spirit, feeling, conception, heart. With *kotoba,* one of the two basic terms used by Japanese court poets and critics. *Kokoro* embraces aspects of tone, treatment, theme, and emotion. It is often used in phrases like *kokoro ari* (conviction of feeling) or *kokoro naki* (without "heart"); the term *ushin* (possessing *kokoro*) is also used, especially to designate a distinct style.

KOTOBA: Materials, diction, words. With *kokoro,* one of the two basic terms in Japanese poetics. *Kotoba* included poetic diction, imagery, prosody, syntax, and beauty of phrasing and sound.

KŪ: Emptiness. The Buddhist conception of the Void or unreality of phenomena and material things.

MAKURAKOTOBA: Pillow-word. A conventional attribute for a word, usually occupying a short 5 syllable line and modifying a word, usually the first in the next line. Pillow-words are often unclear or ambiguous in meaning, and usually carry some imagistic or rhetorically amplifying potential.

MICHI: The Buddhist Way, hence also poetry as a religious way of life. See *shikan*.

MIYABI: Courtliness, elegance. The aesthetic ideal of life during the court tradition and particularly in the early classical period. In poetry, it meant an avoidance of the ugly and a tradition of decorous diction and good taste. See *fūryū*.

MONOGATARI: Tale, romance. Prose fiction, usually incorporating poems. See *utamonogatari, kashū*.

MONO NO AWARE: See *aware*.

NIKKI: (1) Personal journals, often set down in Chinese. (2) Art diaries, fictional or semi-fictional works, usually incorporating poems as a major element. See *kashū*.

NŌ: A dramatic form that took full form during the fourteenth century but flourished a century or two later. Also called *sarugaku no nō* or *dengaku* in early times; today also *yōkyoku*. Many of its themes, ideals, and materials of language derived from court poetry.

NORITO: Shinto liturgy.

RENGA: Linked verse. A form dating from about the thirteenth century; several authors would compose a sequence, usually of a hundred sections or stanzas, alternating 5, 7, 5 syllable lines with 7, 7 syllable units, any two of which formed a complete poem. See *haikai, hyakushuuta*.

SABI: Loneliness. Tone of sadness and desolation prized by mid-classical poets and primarily used to describe a mood, but also associated with images of a withered, monochromatic nature.

SAMA: Style. Term used by Tsurayuki to suggest elegant style, the ideal of the early classical period.

SEDŌKA: Head-repeated poem. A poem of 6 lines, or two tercets—5, 7, 7, 5, 7, 7 syllables—often used for dialogue. A rare form, with few surviving examples of major literary interest.

SHIKAN: Concentration and insight, a religious discipline taught in

Tendai Buddhism and adapted to poetic composition by some mid-classical poets. See *michi*.

SHINKU: See *soku*.

SOKU: Distantly related verses. Poem in which upper and lower verses were seemingly unrelated. Innovating poets of the late classical period often preferred this form to *shinku* (verses closely related by imagery and rhetorical techniques). These differences in preference were reflected in the techniques of integrating anthologies, and they later influenced the *renga* poets.

SONZAI: Existence. Buddhist conception of transient human and natural life.

SUKUSE: Karma. Buddhist conception of causation, holding that a person's destiny in this life is determined by his actions in an earlier existence. Sometimes regarded as the essential feature of the Law (*nori*), the teachings of the Buddha.

TABI: Travel away from the capital, expressed in poetry as sadness tinged with beauty; a subject of poetry from the early classical period.

TAKETAKASHI: Lofty in style; *taketakaki yō,* the lofty style, applying primarily to poems of nature, describing subjects with decorous directness.

TANKA: "Short poem" of 31 syllables in 5 lines: 5, 7, 5, 7, 7. Used also as an envoy to the *chōka* and as a semi-discrete unit in sequences. It is the major form of Japanese court poetry.

TSUKURIMONOGATARI: Fictional tales, of which the *Tale of Genji* is the greatest; usually a prose narrative containing poems. (Differentiated from *jiroku monogatari,* or narratives largely factual.)

USHIN: Conviction of feeling, referring to a specific style designated by Teika and stressing passion. See *kokoro.*

UTAAWASE: Poetry match. A contest of poems matched on stated topics (*dai*) between poets arrayed on two sides and competing before judges. At first a pastime, such matches later became highly serious occasions demanding most considered art and affording poets with opportunities to display their powers in formal verse. See *jikaawase.*

UTAKOTOBA: Poetic diction. See *kotoba.*

UTAMONOGATARI: Tales of poems. Collections of poems with prose contexts, usually fictionalized but purportedly based on true events. Most important example is the *Ise Monogatari.* See *monogatari.*

WAKA: Sometimes used as synonym for *tanka*. Also signifies court poetry in forms including *tanka, chōka,* and *sedōka* in contrast to popular songs or religious hymns. Also used in a very general sense to mean all poetry written in Japanese.

YŌEMBI: Ethereal beauty expressive of romance and delicate shadings, and referring to a style used especially by Teika in his early years, involving complex techniques and an aura of magic.

YŪGEN: Mystery and depth. An ideal of the mid-classical period and particularly of Shunzei; also the name for a style associated with *sabi* and expressive of desolation and rich mysterious beauty coupled with sadness. Subsequently redefined in *nō* and *haikai*.

ZŌ: Miscellaneous. A category of poems in which no one element (e.g., love, a season) dominated to the exclusion of others.

Finding List for Poems

The poems are given here in their sequence within a collection or other source. The collections and sources are: *Man'yōshū*; imperial collections in chronological sequence; *Nikki* (diaries) and *Monogatari* (tales) as in *Kokka Taikan*; primitive songs numbered as in Tsuchihashi and Konishi, *Kodai Kayōshū*; collections in *Kokka Taikei*, *Gunsho Ruijū*, and *Zoku Gunsho Ruijū*. For the last three, poems are cited by volume and page; otherwise poems are cited by book (or scroll) number and number of poem. Following these numbers there is the line—the first when the whole poem is given in this book, the first of the passage when only the passage is given. The final number(s) in each entry refers to the page(s) on which the poem appears.

Man'yōshū

I. 1. Ko mo yo, 37–38
  16. Fuyugomori, 38
  29. Tamatasuki, 46
  30. Sasanami no, 47
  31. Sasanami no, 47
  32. Inishie no, 56
II. 135. Tsunosahau, 51–52
  136. Aogoma no, 52
  137. Akiyama ni, 52
  199. Kakemaku mo, 40–44
  200. Hisakata no, 44
  201. Haniyasu no, 44
  220. Tamamo yoshi, 48–49, 148
  221. Tsuma mo araba, 49
  222. Okitsunami, 49
III. 273. Iso no saki, 56
  305. Kaku yue ni, 56
  318. Tago no ura yu, 68
V. 804. Yo no naka no, 63–64
  805. Tokiwa nasu, 64
  892. Kaze majie, 59–61

893. Yo no naka o, 61
905. Wakakereba, 58
VI. 923. Yasumishishi, 68
  924. Mi-Yoshino no, 68
  925. Nubatama no, 69, 147
  1001. Masurao wa, 5, 67
VII. 1068. Ame no umi ni, 54
IX. 1800. Okakitsu no, 57
XVIII. 4094. Tōtsu kamuoya no, 72
XIX. 4139. Haru no sono, 78
  4140. Waga sono no, 77
  4214. Ame tsuchi no, 73–75
  4215. Tōto ni mo, 75
  4216. Yo no naka no, 75
  4290. Haru no no ni, 76
  4291. Waga yado no, 77
  4292. Uraura ni, 77
XX. 4360. Unabara mireba, 5

Kokinshū

I. 22. Kasugano no, 24
  38. Kimi narade, 10
  53. Yo no naka ni, 151

II. 84. Hisakata no, 91
90. Furusato to, 148
113. Hana no iro wa, 84
117. Yadori shite, 94
III. 139. Satsuki matsu, 99, 119
160. Samidare no, 93
V. 262. Chihayaburu, 148
VI. 329. Yuki furite, 14
IX. 409. Honobono to, 99
XII. 615. Inochi ya wa, 91
XIII. 616. Oki mo sezu, 86
645. Kimi ya koshi, 85
646. Kakikurasu, 15, 85
656. Utsutsu ni wa, 83
658. Yumeji ni wa, 83
667. Shita ni nomi, 91
XIV. 681. Yume ni dani, 95
XV. 747. Tsuki ya aranu, 87, 153
791. Fuyugare no, 95
797. Iro miede, 82
XVI. 838. Asu shiranu, 92
861. Tsui ni yuku, 86
XVIII. 971. Toshi o hete, 25
972. No to naraba, 25
XIX. 1030. Hito ni awan, 82

Shūishū

IV. 224. Omoikane, 94
XX. 1342. Kuraki yori, 96

Goshūishū

I. 43. Kokoro aran, 112
XIII. 755. Kurogami no, 95
763. Arazaran, 95

Senzaishū

IV. 258. Yū sareba, 25, 109
XX. 1275. Fukaku irite, 149

Shinkokinshū

I. 16. Sazanami ya, 7
36. Miwataseba, 104
38. Haru no yo no, 114
45. Ume ga ka ni, 117
II. 112. Kaze kayou, 120
149. Hana wa chiri, 118

III. 202. Ame sosogu, 108
245. Tachibana no, 119
IV. 291. Fushimiyama, 109
361. Sabishisa wa, 17, 117
362. Kokoro naki, 103, 106, 153
363. Miwataseba, 13, 104
420. Samushiro ya, 113
V. 472. Kirigirisu, 112
VI. 625. Tsu no kuni no, 112
670. Sabishisa o, 30n
671. Koma tomete, 30n, 115
672. Matsu hito no, 30n
673. Yume kayou, 30n, 121
VIII. 796. Mare ni kuru, 109
X. 953. Tabibito no, 115
957. Furusato mo, 120
961. Fushiwabinu, 121
964. Makura tote, 117
XI. 1034. Tama no o yo, 118
1074. Shirube se yo, 118
XIV. 1335. Kayoikoshi, 120
XVII. 1599. Hito sumanu, 7
XVIII. 1810. Akatsuki no, 119

Shinchokusenshū

I. 57. Omokage ni, 110

Gyokuyōshū

I. 83. Ume no hana, 128
III. 419. Eda ni moru, 26
V. 684. Onozukara, 133
819. Nobe tōki, 132
VIII. 1239. Kajimakura, 136
XII. 1702. Higoro yori, 133
1707. Yowarihatsuru, 131, 136
XIII. 1768. Tsuraki amari, 132
XV. 2172. Hibikikuru, 134

Fūgashū

II. 189. Hana no ue ni, 131
IV. 398. Matsu o harau, 130
VI. 563. Inazuma no, 13
566. Nioi shirami, 134
VII. 664. Someyaranu, 127, 136
VIII. 794. Furiharuru, 129
XI. 1036. Kurenikeri, 26
XIII. 1297. Waga kokoro, 127

XIV. 1355. Itoioshimi, 130
XVI. 1764. Ato mo naki, 126
XVIII. 2057. Mado no to ni, 135

Nikki in *Kokka Taikan*
No. 4. Aru mono to, 93
No. 41. Wasuregai, 15
No. 56. Amagumo no, 6
No. 449. Fureba yo no, 23
No. 506. Tamakura no, 96
No. 561. Koishikuba, 10

Monogatari in *Kokka Taikan*
No. 146. Koishikuba, 10
No. 221. Toshi o hete, 25
No. 222. No to naraba, 25

Primitive Poems and Songs
Kojiki. No. 49. Susukori ga, 12
No. 58. Tsuginefu ya, 12
Nihongi. No. 54. Tsuginefu ya, 12
Azumaasobiuta. No. 8. Ōhire ya, 13
Kagura. No. 47. Ame naru hibari,
12

Collections in *Kokka Taikei*
Kokin Rokujō. IX, 264. Fukikure-
ba, 92

Akishino Gesseishū. XI, 98. Yama-
to ka mo, 7
Sankashū. XI, 255. Tou hito mo,
111
Shūgyokushū. X, 740. Kajimakura,
121
Shūi Gusō. XI, 389. Haru kureba,
103
XI, 450. Shitaogi mo, 116
XI, 452. Hajime yori, 116

Collections in *Gunsho Ruijū*
Michiyukiburi. XVIII, 559. Mono-
nofu no, 138
XVIII, 560. Uchikawasu, 138
XVIII, 566. Ōzaki no, 137
Sōgi Hōshi Shū. XV, 480. Yo o sa-
mumi, 142
XV, 482. Tsuki wa mada, 142
XV, 489. Yume sasou, 143

Collections in *Zoku Gunsho Ruijū*
Shōtetsu Hyakushu. XXVIII, 906.
Tachibana no, 140
XXVIII, 907. Nakagaki no, 139
XXVIII, 911. Ukareyuku, 139
Shinkei Sōin Hyakushu. XXVIII,
914. Mushi no koe, 141
XXVIII, 914. Sate mo mi ni, 141

Index

Abutsu, Nun, 124
Akahito. *See* Yamabe Akahito
Akiko, Empress, 97–98
Allusive variation (*honkadori*), 24–26, 162
Annual Ceremonial (*nenchūgyōji*), 8, 28
Antony and Cleopatra, 152
Ariie. *See* Fujiwara Ariie
Aristotle, 153
Ariwara Narihira (825–80), 24–27 *passim*, 81–94 *passim*, 99, 106–8, 113, 117, 136, 155; poems by, 14–15, 25, 150. *See also Tales of Ise*
Arnold, Matthew, 76
Ashikaga Yoshinori, 8
Asukai Masayo (1390–1452), 142
Aware, 10–11, 16, 161

Bashō. *See* Matsuo Bashō
Buddhism, 3, 14f, 31, 82–90 *passim*, 96, 103–7 *passim*, 114, 119, 129–30, 135, 141, 146–56 *passim*. *See also* Tendai Buddhism; Zen Buddhism
Bunya Yasuhide (fl. ca. 870), 81
Bureau of Song (*wakadokoro*), 81
Buson. *See* Yosa Buson

Catullus, 145
Celebration, as theme, 11–17 *passim*, 70, 90, 153–54, 159
Charm (*en*), 102, 108, 161
Chikako, Lady Jusammi, 128, 132–33
China, heritage of, 21, 32, 38–39, 54f, 61–62, 82, 93, 144–45
Chōka, 22, 27, 88, 161
Chokusenshū, 4, 161
Chōmei. *See* Kamo no Chōmei

Collection of Ancient and Modern
Times. *See Kokinshū*
Confucianism, 3, 61–62
Conventions of court poetry, 18–35; *see also* Allusive variation; Engo; Pillowword; Pivot-word
Conviction of feeling (*ushin*), 163
Courtliness (*miyabi*), 3, 163
Court poetry: human feeling in, 9–12; forms and techniques of, 18–35; language of, 19–21; major themes of, 144–59
Courtly values, 1–17
Cumberland, Richard, 85n

Dai. See Topic
Darumauta, 126, 161
Desolation, as theme, 11–17 *passim*, 90, 153–57, 159
Diaries (*nikki*), 28, 161f; as art form, 155
Diary of Izumi Shikibu (Izumi Shikibu Nikki), 10, 14, 20, 23, 28, 80, 95–98 *passim*
Diary of the Waning Moon (Isayoi Nikki), 124
Donne, John, 61
Dr. Zhivago, 27
Dream, as metaphor for love, 152–53
Dryden, John, 50

Early classical period (784–1100), 79–100
Early literary period (686–784), 36–78
Eifuku, Empress (1271–1342), 26, 127n, 128, 130–36 *passim*
Eifuku Mon'in, Lady (fl. ca. 1310), 127
Eiga Taigai, 34
Eliot, Sir Charles, 130n

Eliot, T. S., 51
Emerson, Ralph Waldo, 1
Emptiness. *See* Void
En, 102, 108, 161
Engo, 121, 161
Essential nature. *See* Hon'i
Ethereal beauty. *See* Yōembi; En

Fictional tales (*tsukurimonogatari*), 27, 80, 164
Freud, Sigmund, 152
Fūgashū, 125, 137, 157
Fujiwara Ariie (1155–1216), 29–30, 118
Fujiwara Ietaka (1158–1237), 117
Fujiwara Kunifusa (fl. ca. 1080), 29–30
Fujiwara Shunzei (1114–1204), 32–35 *passim,* 101, 108–12, 117, 121–25 *passim,* 140; poems by, 7, 25
Fujiwara style, 100
Fujiwara Tameie (1198–1275), 124f, 127n
Fujiwara Teika (1162–1241), 11, 34–35, 102–8 *passim,* 112–25 *passim,* 128, 132f, 139–44 *passim,* 158n; poems by, 13, 29–30
Fujiwara Teika's Superior Poems of Our Time, 158n
Fujiwara Yoshitsune (1169–1206), 6–7
Fundamentals of Poetic Composition (Eiga Taigai), 34; *see also* Fujiwara Teika
Fūryū, 3, 161; *see also* Miyabi
Fushimi, Emperor (1265–1317), 128, 133–37 *passim*

Genji Monogatari. See Tale of Genji
Go-Daigo, Emperor, 5
Go-Hanazono, Emperor, 8
Gosenshū, 27, 34n, 100
Goshūishū, 111
Gossamer Diary (Kagerō Nikki), 80, 97
Go-Toba, Emperor (1180–1239), 104f, 108, 112, 117, 125
Gyokuyōshū, 29, 125, 134, 157

Hachidaishū, 161
Hachi no Ki, 115
Haikai, 22, 105, 123, 143, 157, 161; *see also* Renga
Haiku, 27, 30, 80, 105, 162

Hakanasa, 105, 153, 162
Hanazono, Emperor (1297–1348), 125f
Heart. *See* Kokoro
Heike Monogatari (Tale of the Heike), 114
Heizei, Emperor (r. 806–9), 147–48
Henjō, Bishop, 81
Hibbett, Howard, 158n
Hisamatsu Sen'ichi, 139n, 149n
Hitomaro. *See* Kakinomoto Hitomaro
Hitomaro Collection, 54
Homer, 144
Hon'i (essential nature), 6, 113, 116, 162
Honkadori, 24–26, 162
Horace, 11, 144
Human values, 1–17
Hyakunin Isshu, 2
Hyakushuuta, 162

Ietaka. *See* Fujiwara Ietaka
Imagawa Ryōshun (1325–1420), 137–43 *passim*
Imayō (popular songs), 80
Imperial Anthologies (*chokusenshū*), 4, 161
Isayoi Nikki (Diary of the Waning Moon), 124
Ise, Lady (fl. ca. 900), 94–99
Ise Monogatari. See Tales of Ise
Ise, Shrine Priestess of, 85, 89, 152
Iwa, Empress, 37
Izumi Shikibu (ca. 970–ca. 1030), 2, 23, 95–99; *see also* Diary of Izumi Shikibu

Jakuren, Priest (d. 1201), 16–17, 117
Japanese Court Poetry, 36n
Jien, Priest (1155–?1225), 121–22, 137
Jikaawase, 30–31, 162; *see also* Poetry match
Jimmu, Emperor, 45
Jinshin, War of, 40, 45
Jiroku Monogatari, 163; *see also* Monogatari; Tsukurimonogatari
Jitō, Empress, 40
Johnson, Samuel, 146
Jukkai, 8, 161
Junii Tameko, Lady (fl. ca. 1290), 127
Jusammi Chikako, Lady (fl. ca. 1300), 128, 132–33

Kabuki, 16, 28
Kagerō Nikki (Gossamer Diary), 80, 97
Kagura, 11f
Kakekotoba. *See* Pivot-word
Kakinomoto Hitomaro (fl. 680–700), 5, 23, 36–54 *passim*, 58, 81, 107, 148, 154; compared with other poets, 67–76 *passim*, 113
Kami, 11–12
Kamo no Chōmei (1153–1216), 16, 102, 117–18, 140
Karma (*sukuse*), 14, 105, 164; *see also* Law
Kashū, 28, 162
Ki no Tomonori (fl. ca. 890), 10, 17, 81, 90–92, 150
Ki no Tsurayuki (868–945), 9, 18–20 *passim*, 24, 32–35 *passim*, 69, 80–83 *passim*, 88, 92–94, 99ff, 107, 117, 123, 144ff, 158f; poems by, 6, 15, 24, 148
Kin'yōshū, 101
Kisen, Priest, 81
Kojiki, 7, 148
Kokinshū, 6, 8f, 23, 28f, 32, 34n, 69, 80f, 89, 93, 99f, 126, 137, 140, 147n; preface to, 18, 102, 117; *see also* Ki no Tsurayuki
Kokoro, 18–19, 21, 34–35, 83, 110, 161
Komachi. *See* Ono no Komachi
Koretaka, Prince, 85, 88
Kosaibari, 11
Koshikibu, 98
Kotoba, 18–19, 21, 34–35, 162; *see also* Utakotoba
Kū. *See* Void
Kwallŭk, 36
Kyōgoku poets, 123–43 *passim*
Kyōgoku Tamekane (1254–1332), 26, 128–36 *passim*; literary criticism of, 125–28
Kyōgoku Tamenori (1226–79), 124

Lady Ōtomo of Sakanoe, Elder Daughter of, 72, 77
Language, Japanese, 19–21, 79, 144; *see also* Kotoba
Late classical period (1241–1500), 123–43
Law (*nori*), 105; *see also* Karma
Linked verse. *See* Renga

Lofty style (*taketakashi*), 150, 163
Loneliness. *See* Sabi
Lord Tamekane's Poetic Notes, 125
Love, as subject, 151–53

Makurakotoba. *See* Pillow-word
Makura no Sōshi. *See Pillow Book of Sei Shōnagon*
Man, as theme, 150–54, 158
Man'yōshū, 4–8 *passim*, 22, 56, 79, 81, 101, 115, 125, 133, 146; discussion of poets in, 36–78 *passim*
Mather, Cotton, 150
Matsuo Bashō, 105f, 111n, 123, 143, 157, 158n
Michi, 163
Michitsuna, Mother of, 97
Michiyukiburi, 137–38; *see also* Imagawa Ryōshun
Mid-classical period (1100–1241), 101–22 *passim*
Milton, John, 27, 144
Mimosusogawa Utaawase (Poetry Contest at the Mimosuso River), 32
Minamoto Shunrai (?1057–1129), 101
Minamoto Tsunenobu (1016–97), 101
Minase Sangin Hyakuin, 158n
Miscellaneous poems (*zōka*), 165
Miyabi, 3, 163; *see also* Fūryū
Monogatari, 28, 152, 163; *see also* Tsukurimonogatari
Mozart, Wolfgang, 154
Mumyōshō, 16
Murasaki Shikibu, 97–98; *see also Tale of Genji*
Mystery and depth style. *See Yūgen*

Nambōroku, 105
Narihira. *See* Ariwara Narihira
Narrow Road Through the Provinces (Oku no Hosomichi), 106, 111n
Nature, as theme, 146–50, 158
Nenchūgyōji, 8, 28
Nihongi, 7, 148
Nijō poets, 124–25
Nijō Tameuji, 124
Nijō Yoshimoto, 137
Nijūichidaishū ("collections of 21 eras"), 8, 161
Nikki (diaries), 28, 161f
Nō, 28, 115, 162

Nōin, Priest, 112
Nori (Law), 105; *see also* Karma
Norito (Shinto liturgies), 50, 163
Nukata, Princess (fl. ca. 660–90), 38–39, 50

Oku no Hosomichi (*Narrow Road Through the Provinces*), 106, 111n; *see also* Matsuo Bashō
Okura. *See* Yamanoe Okura
Ono no Komachi (fl. ca. 850), 81–90 *passim*, 94f, 99, 118, 120, 132, 136
Ōshikōchi Mitsune (fl. ca. 900), 14
Ōtomo Kanamura, 71
Ōtomo Kuronushi, 81
Ōtomo Suguri, 36–37, 71
Ōtomo Yakamochi (718–85), 5, 37, 58, 69, 71–79, 154

Pillow Book (*Makura no Sōshi*), 28, 80, 97, 104; *see also* Sei Shōnagon
Pillow-word (*makurakotoba*), 22, 24, 96, 163
Pivot-word (*kakekotoba*), 23–24, 162; *see also* Ono no Komachi; Ki no Tsurayuki
Po Chü-i, 135
Poetic diary, 28
Poetic diction. *See Utakotoba*
Poetic sequences, 4, 28–30, 32, 125n, 156; *see also Gyokuyōshū*; *Shinkokinshū*; *Soku*
Poetry Contest at the Mimosuso River (*Mimosusogawa Utaawase*), 32
Poetry match (*utaawase*), 4, 30–32, 164; *see also Jikaawase*
Pope, Alexander, 144
The Potted Tree (*Hachi no Ki*), 115
Primitive songs, 12–13, 21–22
Prosody, 21–22; *see also* Conventions

Quintilian, M. Fabius, 9

Racine, Jean, 86
Reizei poets, 123–43 *passim*
Reizei Tamehide (d. 1372), 13
Reizei Tamesuke, 124
Renga (linked verse), 22, 102, 117, 123, 137, 140–43 *passim*, 157; *see also Haikai*

Ryōshun. *See* Imagawa Ryōshun

Sabi, 103, 112, 114, 117, 163
Saigyō, Priest (1118–90), 31, 103–8 *passim*, 111–12; 121, 132f, 149f, 153
Sama, 82, 90, 92, 163
Sandaishū, 161
Sankashū, 111; *see also* Saigyō, Priest
Sarashina Diary (*Sarashina Nikki*), 97
Sarugaku ("monkey music"), early version of nō, 80
Sasamegoto, 34n; *see also* Shinkei, Bishop
Sedōka, 22, 54, 163
Sei Shōnagon, 97, 98, 104; *see also Pillow Book*
Sen no Rikyū, 105, 107
Shakespeare, William, 1
Shikan, 110, 163
Shinchokusenshū, 123
Shinkei, Bishop (1406–75), 34, 140–42
Shinkokinshū, 29–30, 104, 112–15 *passim*, 123, 153, 156f
Shinku, 164; *see also Soku*; Poetic sequences
Shinshokukokinshū, 8, 142
Shinto, 3, 11, 13f, 50, 69, 146–50; liturgies (*norito*), 50, 163
Shin'yōshū, 125
Shokushi, Princess (d. 1201), 118–20, 136, 142
Shōtetsu Monogatari, 139
Shōtetsu, Priest (1381–1459), 138–40, 142f
Shōtoku, Prince, 3
Shūishū, 34n, 100
Shun'e, Priest, 102
Shunzei. *See* Fujiwara Shunzei
Shunzei, Daughter of (fl. ca. 1200), 118–20, 140
Single Poems of a Hundred Poets (*Hyakunin Isshu*), 2
Six Poetic Geniuses, 81
Sōgi, Priest (1421–1502), 123, 142–43
Sōkonshū, 139; *see also* Shōtetsu, Priest
Soku, 164; *see also Shinku*; Poetic sequences
Sone no Yoshitada, 101
Sora. *See* Void
Styles of Court Poetry. *See Sama*,

Charm, Conviction of Feeling; Fujiwara style; Lofty style; *Yūgen*
Sukuse. See Karma
Sung poetry, 128

Tabi (travel), as topic, 6, 103
Taboos, 47–48
Taira Kiyomori, 5
Takechi Furuhito (dates unknown), 55–56
Takechi Kurohito (dates unknown), 55–56, 58, 70, 138
Takechi, Prince, 40, 45
Taketakashi (lofty style), 150, 163
Taketori Monogatari (*Tale of the Bamboo Cutter*), 80
Tale. *See Monogatari*
Tale of the Bamboo Cutter (*Taketori Monogatari*), 80
Tale of Genji (*Genji Monogatari*), 9, 14, 20, 27, 31n, 80, 83, 97f, 114, 139, 150f, 155, 164
Tale of the Heike (*Heike Monogatari*), 114
Tale of Shōtetsu (*Shōtetsu Monogatari*), 139
Tales of Ise (*Ise Monogatari*), 10, 24, 27, 80, 164
Tales of poems. *See Utamonogatari*; *Tales of Ise*
Tamekane. *See* Kyōgoku Tamekane
Tamekane Kyō Wakashō, 126n, 127n; *see also* Kyōgoku Tamekane
Tameko, Lady Junii, 127
Tanabe Sakimaro (ca. 750), 56–58
Tanka, 22, 27, 54, 88, 163
Taoism, 3
Teika. *See* Fujiwara Teika
Temmu, Emperor, 40
Tendai Buddhism, 110; *see also* Buddhism; *Shikan*
Tenji, Emperor, 38–39, 40
Themes of court poetry, 144–59; *see also* Celebration; Desolation; Man; Nature; Time
Thomas, Dylan, 18–19
Time, as theme, 154–59
Tomonori. *See* Ki no Tomonori
Topic (*dai*), 33, 161; *see also* Love, *Tabi*

Tosa Diary (*Tosa Nikki*), 6, 9, 15, 28, 32f, 80, 93, 149f, 155; *see also* Ki no Tsurayuki
Transience. *See Hakanasa*
Travel. *See Tabi*
Travelings (*Michiyukiburi*), 137–38
Tristan and Iseult, 152
Tsukurimonogatari (fictional tales), 27, 80, 164; *see also Monogatari*
Tsunoda, Ryusaku, 34n, 36n
Tsurayuki. *See* Ki no Tsurayuki

Ushin, 163
Utaawase. *See* Poetry match
Utakotoba, 3, 21, 164
Utamonogatari, 27, 80, 164; *see also Monogatari*; *Tales of Ise*

Values, 1–17; *see also* Celebration; Desolation; Themes
Virgil, 144
Void (*kū, sora*), 114, 119, 129, 162

Waka, 1, 137n, 140, 165
Waley, Arthur, 9, 96, 98; *see also Tale of Genji*
Wordsworth, William, 9, 35, 76, 105

Yakamochi. *See* Ōtomo Yakamochi
Yamabe Akahito (d. ?736), 4f, 58, 67–72, 81, 89, 108, 147
Yamanoe Okura (?660–?733), 58–67, 69ff, 76
Yasuda, Kenneth, 158n
Yōembi (ethereal beauty), 102, 165; *see also En*
Yokoyama, Masako, 19–20
Yosa Buson, 158n
Yosami, wife of Hitomaro (dates unknown), 39
Yoshitsune. *See* Fujiwara Yoshitsune
Yūgen, 16, 102f, 108f, 112, 114, 117, 140; *see also* Fujiwara Shunzei
Yūryaku, Emperor, 37–38

Zen Buddhism, 14, 126, 128, 133, 136; *see also* Buddhism; *Darumauta*
Zeugma, 26
Zō, 165